T0360515

LIVING THE CORPORATE PURPOSE

Insights from
Companies in Asia

LIVING THE CORPORATE PURPOSE

| Insights from Companies in Asia |

Mark Chong
Flocy Joseph

Singapore Management University, Singapore

World Scientific

EW JERSEY · LONDON · SINGAPORE · BEIJING · SHANGHAI · HONG KONG · TAIPEI · CHENNAI · TOKYO

Published by

World Scientific Publishing Co. Pte. Ltd.

5 Toh Tuck Link, Singapore 596224

USA office: 27 Warren Street, Suite 401-402, Hackensack, NJ 07601

UK office: 57 Shelton Street, Covent Garden, London WC2H 9HE

British Library Cataloguing-in-Publication Data
A catalogue record for this book is available from the British Library.

LIVING THE CORPORATE PURPOSE
Insights from Companies in Asia

ISBN 978-981-122-121-7 (hardcover)
ISBN 978-981-122-122-4 (ebook for institutions)
ISBN 978-981-122-123-1 (ebook for individuals)

For any available supplementary material, please visit
https://www.worldscientific.com/worldscibooks/10.1142/11855#t=suppl

Desk Editor: Sandhya Venkatesh

Typeset by Stallion Press
Email: enquiries@stallionpress.com

Printed in Singapore

Foreword

Ho Kwon Ping

The Covid-19 pandemic has forced most businesses to critically assess what they need to do to survive and support their employees, customers and communities. I firmly believe that businesses that want to do well in this new world need to have a single-minded focus on organizational purpose.

The most sustainable businesses are driven by a deeper purpose — to create value for itself, its stakeholders and society at large. While profit is the fuel that keeps businesses going, it is purpose that provides a destination, a roadmap, and a compass.

When we founded Banyan Tree 25 years ago, we placed sustainability at the core of strategy even before it became a buzzword. Our motto — "embracing the environment, empowering people" — reflects a balanced approach that emphasizes the greater good and a work environment that brings out the best in people. This has not changed. While the hospitality industry (along with others) has been hit hard by the crisis, we are adapting to the new realities and building our resilience. Purpose has been our constant guide.

To be a truly purpose-driven company is to put purpose at the heart of every decision you make. It requires concerted investment and commitment, through both good times and hard times. In this crisis, businesses and their leaders have a choice to re-imagine and build something better, to leave a legacy that balances profit with the greater good. Purpose can be their "North Star".

Mark Chong's and Flocy Joseph's book is a timely one. The book's "3As" framework provides business leaders with a road-map on articulating, assimilating and activating their organisational purpose. Discovering and articulating a company's purpose is the first thing a company needs to do. Once that is achieved, it needs to scale purpose from its founding days to beyond and bring it alive for thousands of people, across multiple locations. Finally, it needs to engage other stakeholders to activate its purpose beyond the company so that it achieves broader societal impact.

The book also tells the stories of 13 purpose-driven companies and the different approaches they have taken in articulating, assimilating and activating their purpose. Importantly, these stories address how the companies are responding to Covid-19. At a time when fear and uncertainty complicate efforts in speaking about purpose, these stories show how the companies have brought their people along.

Finally, the book issues a series of practical calls to action that is based on lessons distilled from the journeys of the 13 featured companies.

Anyone working in a business can take something out of the framework, case studies and calls to action contained in this book. *Living the Corporate Purpose* can inspire and guide your company's purpose-driven journey — wherever you happen to be on it.

Ho Kwon Ping

Executive Chairman, Banyan Tree Holdings and
Laguna Resorts and Hotels
Executive Chairman, Thai Wah Public Company
Chairman, Board of Trustees, Singapore Management University

Introduction

The principle of shareholder value maximization has dominated capitalism and corporate boardrooms for 50 years. While it has brought the world significant benefits, it has not been able to convincingly address deeply troubling issues such as climate change and income inequality (Gast *et al.*, 2020). Furthermore, it has often come at the expense of other stakeholders and resulted in popular distrust of big business. Thus, the notion that a firm's purpose is "just making money" — attributed to the economist Milton Friedman — is increasingly being discredited (Mayer, 2020). In fact, just seven percent of Fortune 500 CEOs believe their companies should "mainly focus on making profits and not be distracted by social goals" (Murray, 2019).

In August 2019, the Business Roundtable — the largest business association in the US — redefined the goal of business as one that promotes the interests of all stakeholders, such as those of employees, customers, suppliers, communities and shareholders. The act was seen as the business community's acknowledgement of its responsibilities towards society — i.e. to generate and share wealth more sustainably and evenly. It also reflects a (belated) recognition that a corporation's licence to operate is given by its stakeholders (The Editorial Board, 2019).

In December 2019, the World Economic Forum issued a new manifesto spelling out "The Universal Purpose of a Company in the Fourth Industrial Revolution" (Schwab, 2019). The manifesto makes clear that the traditional focus on shareholder value is neither fair nor right; neither can it meet the challenges of the 21st century (Mayer, 2020; Schwab, 2019). Instead, a business should revolve around its purpose — the reason it exists, what it sets out to do and what it aspires to be (Mayer, 2020). It follows that a business' practices and policies should emanate from that purpose. More specifically, corporate purpose should be "to produce profitable solutions to the problems of people and the planet, and not to profit from producing problems for people or the planet. It is about precise descriptions of what problems companies are solving, for whom, how, when and why they are best suited to do that" (Mayer, 2020).

These discussions of corporate purpose are happening at a time when trust in institutions — including business — is very low. This distrust is fueled by a myriad of factors including a growing sense of inequity, pessimism about economic prospects and lack of confidence in leaders. The 2020 Edelman Trust Barometer shows that while trust is built on a combination of competence and ethics, no institution — including business — is currently seen by stakeholders as being both competent and ethical. Yet, ethical drivers are three times more important to trust in companies than competence. In addition, 87% of the Edelman survey respondents say that stakeholders, not shareholders, are most important to long-term company success; 73% say that a company can take actions that both increase profits and improve conditions in communities where it operates. The world has also seen the emergence of belief-driven buyers, who will choose, switch, avoid and boycott a brand based on its stand on societal issues (Edelman Trust Barometer 2020).

Employees also increasingly desire for meaning at work: 82% of the more than 1000 participants in a McKinsey survey affirmed the importance of purpose at the workplace. Yet, only 42% reported that their companies' purpose statements drove impact. The survey participants also named "creating meaningful work" among the top two employee priorities. Yet, "creating meaningful work" is the focus of just 11% of purpose statements (Gast *et al.*, 2020).

In Asia, nine in 10 consumers want brands to get involved in the issues they care about. Moreover, 60% of those surveyed said they were more likely to buy brands that are aligned with their views and pay "a little more" for brands with sustainability credentials (Kantar, 2018).

Asian consumers also expect brands to give precedence to relevant local issues, the most important of which are health, well-being (or ending poverty), quality education and hunger in emerging markets, and decent work and economic growth in developed markets. In addition, they believe that brands play an important role in advancing these issues through educating consumers, initiating and funding programs to support the issue, and providing direct funding to other organizations that champion these issues (Kantar, 2018).

There is already ample evidence of a business case for corporate purpose. According to a study by Raj Sisodia and colleagues (2014), purpose-led companies significantly outperformed the S&P 500 between 1996 and 2011. In another study by PwC's Strategy&, more than 90% of purpose-driven companies deliver growth and profits at or above the industry average (Blount & Leinwand, 2019). Moreover, 63% of the 2,000 academic studies that have examined the impact of environmental, social, and governance propositions on returns to equity found positive results (Henisz *et al.*, 2019).

Purpose is also critical to high business growth: research shows that high-growth companies are ones that have moved purpose to the core of their strategy (Malnight *et al.*, 2019). When purpose is backed by committed leadership and financial investment, it empowers the company to create sustainable growth in profits, maintain its relevance and strengthen relationships with its stakeholders (Malnight *et al.*, 2019).

According to the research conducted by the Reputation Institute and StrawberryFrog, consumers are far more likely to recommend the top purpose-driven brands to others, buy products and services of these brands, and work for the company behind these brands. In addition, they would give the benefit of the doubt if a purpose-driven company were facing a crisis (www.purposepowerindex.com).

In the workplace, purpose-driven employees have been found to have higher levels of engagement and personal fulfilment; they also outperform their peers in every indicator, according to the most extensive global study on the role of purpose in the workforce (LinkedIn, 2016). This shouldn't be surprising – people are significantly more motivated by how their firm improves lives (i.e. its transcendent purpose) than by how it sells products and services (Zak, 2014).

Ultimately, companies that demonstrate a credible, enduring commitment to making profits from addressing societal and environmental problems can build long-term trust and loyalty in its stakeholders, and corporate cultures that build a shared identity around a clear purpose will play a key role in establishing that commitment (Mayer, 2020; Schwab, 2019).

Since 2010, "purpose" has appeared in the titles of more than 400 new business and leadership books and in thousands of articles and become a management watchword (Blount & Leinwand, 2019). Even before COVID-19, the world was already facing significant challenges, such as climate change, natural resource depletion and unequal levels of socioeconomic development. But the sheer magnitude of the health and economic crisis is confronting corporate leaders with the question of their *raison detre* — their reason for being — and the impact they are making (or not) on the world.

Now is arguably the best time for purpose-driven businesses, as COVID-19 presents unprecedented opportunities to leverage purpose to benefit stakeholders, especially those with acute needs. More specifically, the crisis allows corporations to bring their greatest strengths to bear on problems and to involve their employees in solutions, thereby building a shared sense of purpose (McKinsey, 2020). In fact, many companies across the world have been inspired by – and amplifying – their purpose at a time when it is needed the most by their stakeholders. Ultimately, a focus on purpose provides companies with an aspirational goal that brings out the best of what a business can be:

> "…providing stewardship of resources which reduces the inefficiency and cost of repairing, restoring or paying for resources unnecessarily consumed in the production of goods and services; showing authentic respect for the whole person in creating a committed workforce, loyal customers, and supportive governments and regulatory agencies; operating freely and responsibly to create new goods and services that society wants; demonstrating empathy toward communities that provide new markets and customers; crossing borders seamlessly to attract the best talent and grow new markets; building long-term relationships that foster loyalty and trust rather than mistrust and its associated costs; and nurturing decision-making that engages with the workforce to encourage innovation and take responsibility for keeping the company true to its purpose" (Hollensbe *et al.*, 2014, p. 1232).

This book is among the very first to study the purpose-driven journeys of corporations in Asia. It starts with a chapter on the "3As" (Articulate, Assimilate and Activate) framework that provides the unifying principles underlying these journeys. Next, the book features 13 companies in Asia that are living their respective corporate purposes — these companies comprise indigenous Asian enterprises as well as US and European multinationals with significant operations in Asia. They represent a broad spectrum of industries — agri-business, banking, consumer packaged goods, infrastructure, insurance, logistics, medical technology, nutrition, paint and coating, software, water and housing products — and different stages of the evolution of organizational purpose. And they fit the four factors that determine if a company is purpose-driven or not:

- Is the company committed to changing the world for the better?
- Does it do things to benefits stakeholders, not just shareholders?
- Does it have a higher purpose that's bigger than profit?
- Does it do things to improve the lives of people and communities? (www.purposepowerindex.com).

The concluding chapter of the book distills key lessons from these 13 companies into calls to action that can guide corporations on how to articulate, assimilate and activate their own purpose.

REFERENCES

Barton, R., Ishikawa, M., Quiring, K., and Theofilu, B. (2018). From me to we: The rise of the purpose-led brand. Accenture. Available at: https://www.accenture.com/us-en/insights/strategy/brand-purpose?c=strat_competitiveagilnovalue_10437227&n=mrl_1118.

Blount, S. and Leinwand, P. (2019). Why are we here? *Harvard Business Review*, 97(6), 132–139.

Blount, S. and Leinwand, P. (2020). In a crisis, companies must know their purpose. *strategy+business*. Available at: https://www.strategy-business.com/article/In-a-crisis-companies-must-know-their-purpose?gko=5a4a1.

Business Roundtable redefines the purpose of a corporation to promote "an economy that serves all Americans". (2019). Business Roundtable. Available at: https://www.businessroundtable.org/business-roundtable-redefines-the-purpose-of-a-corporation-to-promote-an-economy-that-serves-all-americans.

Edelman Trust Barometer (2020). Edelman. Available at: https://www.edelman.com/sites/g/files/aatuss191/files/2020-01/2020%20Edelman%20Trust%20Barometer%20Global%20Report_LIVE.pdf.

Gast, A., Illanes, P., Probst, N., Schaninger, B., & Simpson, B. (2020). Purpose: Shifting from why to how. *McKinsey Quarterly*. Available at: https://www.mckinsey.com/business-functions/organization/our-insights/purpose-shifting-from-why-to-how

Henisz, W., Koller, T., & Nuttall, R. (2019). Five ways that ESG creates value. *McKinsey Quarterly*. Available at: https://www.mckinsey.com/business-functions/strategy-and-corporate-finance/our-insights/five-ways-that-esg-creates-value

Hollensbe, E., Wookey, C., Hickey, L., George, G., and Nichols, V. (2014). Organizations with purpose: From the editors. *Academy of Management Journal*, 57(5), 1227–1234.

Kantar (2018). *Purpose in Asia*. Available at: https://go.tnsglobal.com/kantar-purpose-in-asia-2018.

LinkedIn (2016). *2016 Workforce purpose index. Purpose at work*. Available at: https://cdn.imperative.com/media/public/Global_Purpose_Index_2016.pdf.

Malnight, T.W., Buche, I., and Dhanaraj, C. (2019). Put purpose at the core of your strategy. *Harvard Business Review*. Available at: https://hbr.org/2019/09/put-purpose-at-the-core-of-your-strategy.

Mayer, C. (2020). It's time to redefine the purpose of business. Here's a roadmap. World Economic Forum. Available at: https://www.weforum.org/agenda/2020/01/its-time-for-a-radical-rethink-of-corporate-purpose/.

Murray, A. (2020). The Fortune 500 CEO Survey Results Are In. *Fortune. com.* Available at: https://fortune.com/2019/05/16/fortune-500-2019-ceo-survey/

Schwab, K. (2019). *Davos Manifesto 2020: The universal purpose of a company in the Fourth Industrial Revolution (2020).* World Economic Forum. Available at: https://www.weforum.org/agenda/2019/12/davos-manifesto-2020-the-universal-purpose-of-a-company-in-the-fourth-industrial-revolution/.

Sisodia, R., Sheth, J.N., & Wolfe, D. (2014). *Firms of endearment: How world-class companies profit from passion and purpose.* Pearson Education.

The Editorial Board (2019). Business must act on a new corporate purpose. *Financial Times.* Available at: https://www.ft.com/content/3732eb04-c28a-11e9-a8e9-296ca66511c9.

Zak, P. (2014). Why your brain loves good storytelling. *Harvard Business Review.* Available at: https://hbr.org/2014/10/why-your-brain-loves-good-storytelling.

About the Authors

Dr. Mark Chong is Associate Professor of Communication Management (Practice) at Singapore Management University. He has helped students at Singapore Management University (SMU) and executives at organizations such as Pernod Ricard, Mondelez, Maersk and Bhutan's Gross National Happiness Commission to communicate with impact. His teaching at SMU has won him several awards, including the SMU Teaching Excellence Honour Roll. He is the co-author of Living the Corporate Purpose: Insights from Companies in Asia (World Scientific Publishing). His previous books include Brainfruit. Turning Creativity into Cash from East to West (McGraw-Hill) and Winning Corporate Reputation Strategies: Lessons from Asia Pacific (McGraw-Hill). Mark received his Ph.D. from Cornell University. Prior to joining academia, he worked for close to a decade in both corporate and consulting roles.

Dr. Flocy Joseph serves as a Programme Director at Singapore Management University where her role encompasses designing, delivering, and facilitating executive development programmes for the university's top tier corporate clients and regional government officials. She has a breadth of experience in delivering cutting edge programmes in the Infrastructure, Maritime, Financial and Technologies sectors, primarily focusing on Singapore and emerging markets such as Bhutan, Myanmar, Thailand, Oman and the UAE. Through her experience she has successfully forged several international partnerships with overseas business schools in Europe, Americas and Asia.

Over the years, Flocy has authored various case studies on leadership, some of which have been published to global recognition. She has also led a research paper on '*Cultural Transformation in the Digital World*', authored an award winning paper on "*Beta Leadership*" and co-authored the book "*Living the Corporate Purpose: Insights from Companies in Asia*". She is also a certified trainer in various Psychometric tools.

Flocy earned her MBA from Madras University in India with Marketing and Foreign Trade as her specialization and commenced her career in India, gaining a blend of academic, consulting and corporate experience. Years later, she pursued her doctorate from the Singapore Management University. Her doctoral thesis was on "*Responsible Leadership: A Behavioural Perspective' as an alternative form of leadership for leaders in the 21st century "* was one of the top downloaded articles from the SMU International Knowledge System in the year 2018.

She lives in Singapore and during her spare time she enjoys cooking, redecorating her home and tending to her garden.

Acknowledgements

Writing a book is much harder than reading it! It was a work trip to Bhutan that got the two of us getting to know each other and listing out the various items on our bucket list. Despite our different backgrounds and different expectations from life, we had one thing in common — to author a book on corporate purpose. Thus began our journey in February 2020 over a cup of coffee in one of Singapore's quaint townhouses where we observed safe distancing principles as we charted the way forward for this book.

Firstly, what got our writing off to a strong start was the framework proposed by Jin Montesano. All the case studies in this book are anchored in Jin's AAA framework on Articulating, Assimilating and Activating purpose in organizations. We are grateful to Jin for letting us use the Triple A framework.

This book wouldn't have been possible without the support of the purpose-driven companies — 13 of them — that have allowed us to share their approaches to purpose as case studies in our book. The interviews with the C-suite leaders from these thirteen companies as well as the support received from their respective corporate communications teams and their personal assistants allowed us to faithfully document their purpose-led journey. Since our interviews were held during the Covid-19 pandemic, we were able to document how these leaders and their organizations were responding to the crisis and how their purpose served them as a North Star. The learnings from those interviews represent invaluable insights.

We would also like to express our special appreciation and thanks to our two reviewers — Prof Gerry George and Mr Pradeep Pant — for their constructive comments and for their encouragement as we worked on this book. We are indebted to Mr Ho Kwon Ping, Chairman of the Board of Trustees of the Singapore Management University and Executive Chairman of Banyan Tree Holdings for penning the foreword. As someone who is passionate about purposeful leadership, Mr Ho found our book meaningful and timely.

We owe an enormous debt of gratitude to our two transcribers, Mr Neville Joseph and Ms Teh Shi Min. They have painstakingly transcribed every word and upheld the confidentiality of our interviews. We hope in some way that the knowledge they have gained will help them as they transition from their student life to a corporate job.

Words cannot express how grateful we are to Sandhya Venkatesh from Scientific Publishing. Her prompt responses to our various queries, and how well she articulated and streamlined the process of getting this book published made it an enjoyable process.

Finally, we wish to thank our friends and family for their encouragement and excitement on hearing us come up with this book; for believing in us; and for being patient with us as we focused on writing this book. We hope you will enjoy reading this book as much as we have enjoyed writing it.

Contents

1. The "3As" Purpose Framework

Our study of the 13 companies featured in this book reveals that all of them share a common organizing framework[1] in living their organizational purposes. This framework has three interlinked components: articulate, assimilate and activate.

ARTICULATE

The first "A" has to do with the definition and articulation of the organization's purpose. "For a company at the beginning of the 'purpose journey, choosing the appropriate purpose and articulating it is a crucial first step" (Hurth *et al.*, 2018, p. 36). Purpose performs the strategic function of linking an organization to its environment while ensuring compatibility with the organization's tradition and history (George *et al.*, 1999). Ideally, a company's purpose converges with its vision, which is a picture of the organization's imagined future (Erickson & Ward, 2015). Both purpose and vision set the boundaries of possible actions for a company's associates and invite them to take ownership of the company's social impact and future (Fairholm, 1991).

A company's purpose may be found at the confluence of its heritage, core competencies and values, and stakeholder expectations (Thompson, 2017). A study (Malnight *et al.*, 2019) states that companies and leaders can use one of two approaches in

---

[1] This framework may be implicit rather than explicit.

developing a purpose: retrospective or prospective. The retrospective approach requires leaders to look back on the company's heritage, its reason for being and codify the elements that make its culture unique. On the other hand, the prospective approach requires company leaders to look forward, assess the global ecosystem in which the company operates and decide on the impact it could make (Malnight *et al.*, 2019). In any case, a company's purpose needs to provide answers to the questions, "Why does the company exist?", "What value does it create, and for whom?" (Kenny, 2016).

The purpose statement is an inspiring expression of the value that the company creates for the stakeholders it is aiming to serve, while making a profit.[2] Author Simon Sinek (2019) suggests that a company should ultimately aspire for a purpose that fulfills the requirements of being a *Just Cause*. That is, it needs to be *for something* (affirmative and optimistic); inclusive (open to everyone who wishes to contribute); service oriented (for the primary benefit of others); idealistic (big, bold and ultimately unachievable); and resilient (able to endure political, technological and cultural change).

Nonetheless, the purpose cannot just be a framed slogan that hangs on the office wall. It needs to be assimilated by the organization.

ASSIMILATE

A well-defined purpose does not necessarily translate into action. In some cases, the purpose statement becomes nothing more than nice-sounding words on a company wall. For purpose to be more

---

[2] On the other hand, a vision statement expresses where the company wants to be in the future, while a mission statement describes what business the company is in (or isn't). Values describe the company's desired culture (Kenny, 2014).

than just window-dressing, a company-wide commitment to the purpose must be fostered (Sidibe, 2020). A deeply assimilated purpose can help everyone in the company understand the "why", the "what" and the "how" of everything they are doing (Malnight *et al.*, 2019).

The second "A" has to do with the integration of purpose into the organization's cultural fabric and its assimilation by all the employees. "Organizational purpose must be deeply and strategically embedded within the firm for it to become part of the organization's identity" (Hurth *et al.*, 2018. p. 37). A fully assimilated purpose does not happen by itself. Instead, it is the outcome of strategic planning and the leadership's commitment to delivery. 93% of executives surveyed for an EY Beacon Institute study (2017) cited the need to embed purpose into the company's culture and behaviors, especially their leaders' goals, strategies and objectives; governance and decision-making processes and systems; and strategic planning processes at all levels.

A recent survey of more than 540 employees worldwide by Strategy& showed that employees who understand and embrace the company's purpose tend to be inspired to do great work that delivers on business goals (Blount & Leinwand, 2019). Purpose was considered to be more than twice as important (on average) as compensation and career advancement. 65% of the same employees said they were passionate about their work, versus 32% at other companies (Blount & Leinwand, 2019). 73% of the respondents in the 2020 Edelman Trust Barometer study expect their prospective employers to offer them the opportunity to shape the future of society (Edelman, 2020).

To achieve shared purpose, organizations must ensure there is shared cognition, which is how different individuals achieve the same understanding of concrete reality (Ensley & Pearce, 2001; Thompson & Fine, 1999; Weick & Roberts, 1993). Research on groups and teams has shown that people tend to develop shared cognition when they share experiences with others (Resnick, 1991, Thompson & Fine, 1999). Training sessions are one example of such shared experience: when people are trained together, they are exposed to similar stimuli at the same time and encode those stimuli together (Moreland, 1999). Working together on joint projects is another example of shared experience (Reagans *et al.*, 2005). They also learn through discussions with one another about others with whom they have worked in the past (Monge & Contractor, 2003). The organization should also engage its employees in a dialogue about what the organizational purpose means to them if it hopes to have the purpose internalized by its employees.

Stories also promote shared cognition (Resnick *et al.*, 1991) and sensemaking (Gabriel, 2000). For example, vivid stories about the future (e.g. "To one day see a city full of hybrid cars") can lead employees working in the same organization to share a similar mental image (Carton *et al.*, 2015) and make sense of its future. In addition, stories can encourage organizational reflection (e.g. "Where are we now?") (Fleming, 2001). Another benefit of stories is that by presenting separate facts as part of a complex whole, important information is more easily learned and remembered by individuals (Shaw *et al.*, 1998). While storytelling is an activity that is typically associated with leaders and leadership (Denning, 2007), an organization's purpose narrative can only cascade through the ranks if it is told and retold by employees as well (Dailey & Browning, 2014).

Getting employees to understand and believe in the company's purpose is not enough — the company needs to embed that purpose into the culture through the encouragement and enactment of desired behaviors (Vallaster & de Chernatony, 2005). This is especially important, as organizations "increasingly compete based on their ability to express who they are and what they stand for" (Schultz *et al.*, 2000, p. 80), and employees inadvertently communicate what the organization stands for through their behavior (Chong, 2007; Kennedy, 1977; Post & Griffin, 1997; Saxton, 1998). Organizations can help their employees to internalize purpose and align their behavior to that purpose through internal communication, training and the allocation of awards and rewards (Ashforth & Mael, 1989; Schein, 1992; Stuart, 1999; de Chernatony, 1999; Andriopoulos & Gotsi, 2001; Chong, 2007). That is why purpose-driven companies need the help of their HR departments to tie reward and recognition to delivering on their purpose (Sidibe, 2020).

Recent research shows that leaders can also help company members assimilate purpose by creating a context for meaningful collaboration (Cross *et al.*, 2020). In fact, the study indicates that up to half of employees' sense of purpose comes from the quality of their collaborations. This implies that company leaders should help employees see that purpose lies as much in the way they work together as in how they execute the work itself — if not more so (Cross *et al.*, 2020). The same study found that leaders who successfully instill a sense of purpose tend to share ownership early, make shared goals a collaborative undertaking from the start and regularly show appreciation for the work of others (Cross *et al.*, 2020).

Nonetheless, purpose can only be successfully assimilated on a foundation of trust, which enables people to work cooperatively in the pursuit of aspirational goals (Edmondson, 2003). In a high-trust culture, people freely share information and their ideas, have open discussions, and offer their help to others (Edmondson *et al.*,

2020). Company leaders can establish and support the development of trust in a number of ways. They can establish psychological safety, which is the feeling people get when they feel comfortable about offering constructive criticism or new ideas. They can also spend meaningful time in one-on-one meetings with employees and establish personal connections with them (Edmondson *et al.*, 2020).

To achieve social impact, however, a company needs to activate its purpose beyond its own walls.

ACTIVATE

The last "A" has to do with activating and amplifying purpose beyond the organization to achieve social impact. When companies work with public and private partners, they can create a multiplier effect that translates into deeper and broader impact as well as greater efficiency (Sidibe, 2020). In addition, partnerships can confer companies with the moral authority, scale or the learning required to make a meaningful difference (Sidibe, 2020).

Broadly speaking, purpose can be activated in four ways: (1) Generating resources (e.g. money, time, talent); (2) providing choices; (3) influencing mindsets (e.g. through information campaigns) and (4) improving the conditions of stakeholders and society (Vila & Bharadwaj, 2017). These four types of activation may require companies to identify and mobilize various external stakeholders, including those beyond their immediate spheres of influence.

For it to be successful and scalable, a partnership has to be based on an alignment of vision between the partner organizations on addressing a major social or environmental issue; the alignment between the vision and the capabilities each party brings to the partnership is also important (Sidibe, 2020). In addition, the terms of the partnership need to be completely transparent and endorsed at the highest levels of the respective organizations (Sidibe, 2020).

Examples of types of partners	*What to expect?*
NGOs and foundations	Social mobilizations, pooling resources, entry into difficult places and niche programmatic areas
Governments	Access to channels, permissions, lobbying for policy changes
Academia and think tanks	Latest thinking, evidence generation, advocacy and credibility
UN and its agencies	National programmes, expertise, convincing governments
Customers and retailers	Modern trade for cause-related marketing/joint funding and scaling up
Other likeminded private sector organisations	Create social coalitions, bundles in retailers (e.g. Global Handwashing Day/ breakfast deals with fruit/bread

Source: Myriam Sidibe (2020).

A company's existing allies can contribute valuable financial resources, information and expertise, and legitimacy (Kanter, 2020). But the company can also create powerful coalitions comprising several otherwise siloed groups (Kanter, 2020), as purpose provides "an aligning and motivating force for stakeholders to work together to achieve shared outcomes using their unique contributions" (Hurth, p. 17). Finding the right allies and coalition partners can make the difference between success and failure in purpose activation, as they can offer companies complementary and highly valuable resources such as local knowledge, networks and assets.

To bring allies and coalition partners to the same table, and to continue motivating them once they are on board, company leaders should engage in storytelling and become advocates of their corporate purpose (Kanter, 2020). Storytelling is a powerful form of persuasion and motivation because human beings make sense of the world through stories (Turner, 1996). Moreover, stories have been associated with changes in beliefs, attitudes and intentions (van Laer *et al.*, 2014). At its most fundamental level, a story should answer three questions:

- Why are we here?
- What can we accomplish?
- How should we (i.e. the company and its stakeholders) connect in order to accomplish this? (Hagel, 2017).

When a company's purpose is activated through the generation of resources, provision of choices, influencing of mindsets or the improvement of conditions, the media attention, external recognition (e.g. awards) and industry rankings that often ensue act as reputational signals to both internal and external stakeholders (cf. Dhalla, 2007). These independent signals help to validate the company's purpose, thereby reinforcing stakeholders' assessment of the purpose over time (cf. Dhalla, 2007). On the contrary, the absence of positive outcomes can weaken stakeholder assessments of the purpose over time. Thus, it is important for companies to measure what has changed as a result of the activation of its purpose.

As shown in the following diagram, the "3As" are not self-contained, siloed facets but interconnected, iterative and self-reinforcing:

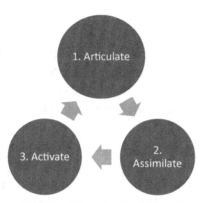

The "3As" Purpose Framework

REFERENCES

Andriopoulos, C. and Gotsi, M. (2001). Living' the corporate identity: Case studies from the creative industry. *Corporate Reputation Review*, 4(2), 144–154.

Ashforth, B.E. and Mael, F. (1989). Social identity theory and the organization. *Academy of Management Review*, 14(1), 20–39.

Blount, S. and Leinwand, P. (2019). Why are we here? *Harvard Business Review*, 97(6), 132–139.

Carton, A.M., Murphy, C., and Clark, J.R. (2015). A (blurry) vision of the future: How leader rhetoric about ultimate goals influences performance. *Academy of Management Journal*, 1015(1), 10–36.

Chong, M. (2007). The role of internal communication and training in infusing corporate values and delivering brand promise: Singapore Airlines' experience. *Corporate Reputation Review*, 10(3), 201–212.

Cross, R., Edmondson, A., and Murphy, W. (2020). A noble purpose alone won't transform your company. *MIT Sloan Management Review*. Available at: https://sloanreview.mit.edu/article/a-noble-purpose-alone-wont-transform-your-company/.

Dailey, S.L. and Browning, L.D. (2014). Retelling stories in organizations: Understanding the functions of narrative repetition. *The Academy of Management Review*, 39(1), 22–43.

de Chernatony, L. (1999). Brand management through narrowing the gap between brand identity and brand reputation. *Journal of Marketing Management*, 15(1–3), 157–179.

Denning, S. (2007). *The secret language of leadership: How leaders inspire action through narrative*. Jossey-Bass.

Dhalla, R. (2007). The construction of organizational identity: Key contributing external and intra-organizational factors. *Corporate Reputation Review*, 10(4), 245–260.

Edelman Trust Barometer (2020). Edelman. Available at: https://www.edelman.com/sites/g/files/aatuss191/files/2020-01/2020%20Edelman%20Trust%20Barometer%20Global%20Report_LIVE.pdf.

Edmondson, A.C. (2003). Managing the risk of learning: Psychological safety in work teams. In M.A. West, D. Tjosvold, and K.G. Smith (Eds.), *International handbook of organizational teamwork and cooperative working* (pp. 255–276). John Wiley & Sons.

Ensley, M.D. and Pearce, C.L. (2001). Shared cognition in top management teams: Implications for new venture performance. *Journal of Organizational Psychology*, 22(2), 145–160.

Erickson, T. and Ward, T. (2015). *The master communicator's handbook*. Changemakers Books.

EY Beacon Institute (2017). How can purpose reveal a path through disruption? Available at: https://www.ey.com/en_sg/purpose/how-can-purpose-reveal-a-path-through-disruption.

Fairholm, G. (1991). *Values leadership: Toward a new philosophy of leadership*. Praeger Publishers.

Fleming, D. (2001). Narrative leadership: Using the power of stories. *Strategy & Leadership*, 29(4). https://doi.org/10.1108/sl.2001.26129dab.002.

Gabriel, Y. (2000). *Storytelling in organizations: Facts, fictions and fantasies*. OUP.

George, G., Sleeth, R.G., and Siders, M.A. (1999). Organizing culture: Leader roles, behaviors, and reinforcement mechanisms. *Journal of Business and Psychology*, 13(4), 545–560.

Hagel, J. (2017). The connection between narrative and purpose. *The Marketing Journal*. Available at: https://www.marketingjournal.org/the-connection-between-narrative-and-purpose-john-hagel/.

Hurth, V., Ebert, C., and Prabhu, J. (2018). Organisational purpose: The construct and its antecedents and consequences. Cambridge Judge Business School Working Paper No. 02/2018.

Kanter, R.M. (2020). *Thinking outside the building: How advanced leaders can change the world one smart innovation at a time*. PublicAffairs.

Kennedy, S.H. (1977). Nurturing corporate images: Total communication or ego trip? *European Journal of Marketing*, 11(3), 120–164.

Kenny, G. (2014). Your company's purpose is not its vision, mission, or values. *Harvard Business Review*, 2–3.

Kenny, G. (2016). Thinking clearly about your company's purpose. *Harvard Business Review*, 2–4.

Malnight, T.W., Buche, I., and Dhanaraj, C. (2019). Put purpose at the core of your strategy. *Harvard Business Review*. Available at: https://hbr.org/2019/09/put-purpose-at-the-core-of-your-strategy.

Monge, P.R. and Contractor, N. (2003). *Theories of communication networks*. Oxford University Press.

Moreland, R.L. (1999). Transactive memory: Learning who knows what in work groups and organizations. In L.L. Thompson, J.M. Levine, and D.M. Messick (Eds.), *LEA's organization and management series. Shared cognition in organizations: The management of knowledge* (pp. 3–31). Lawrence Erlbaum Associates Publishers.

Post, J.E. and Griffin, J.J. (1997). Corporate reputation and external affairs management. *Corporate Reputation Review*, 1(1/2), 165–171.

Reagans, R., Argote, L., and Brooks, D. (2005). Individual experience and experience working together: Predicting learning rates from knowing who knows what and knowing how to work together. *Management Science*, 51(6), 869–881.

Resnick, L.B. (1991). Shared cognition: Thinking as social practice. In L. B. Resnick, J.M. Levine, and S.D. Teasley (Eds.), *Perspectives on socially shared cognition* (pp. 1–20). American Psychological Association.

Resnick, L.B., Levine, J.M., and Teasley, S.D. (Eds.). (1991). *Perspectives on socially shared cognition*. American Psychological Association.

Saxton, K. (1998). Where do reputations come from? *Corporate Reputation Review*, 1(4), 393–399.

Schein, E.H. (1992). *Organizational culture and leadership*, Jossey-Bass.

Shaw, G., Brown, R., and Bromiley, P. (1998). Strategic stories: How 3M is rewriting business planning. *Harvard Business Review*, 76(3), 41–42, 44, 46–50.

Schultz, M., Hatch, M.J., and Larsen, M.H. (2000). *The expressive organization*. Oxford University Press.

Sinek, S. (2019). *The infinite game*. Portfolio.

Stuart, H. (1999). Towards a definitive model of the corporate identity management process. *Corporate Communications: An International Journal*, 4(4), 200–207.

Sidibe, M. (2020). *Brands on a mission: How to achieve social impact and business growth through purpose*. Routledge.

Thompson, A.B. (2017). *Do good: Embracing brand citizenship to fuel both purpose and profit*. AMACOM.

Thompson, L. and Fine, G.A. (1999). Socially shared cognition, affect, and behaviour. *Personality and Social Psychology Review*, 3(4), 278–302.

Turner, M. (1996). *The literary mind: The origins of thought and language*. Oxford University Press.

Vallaster, C. and de Chernatony, L. (2005). Internationalization of services brands: The role of leadership during the internal brand building process. *Journal of Marketing Management*, 21(1/2), 181–203.

van Laer, T., De Ruyter, K., Visconti, L.M., and Wetzels, M. (2014). The extended transportation-imagery model: A meta-analysis of the antecedents and consequences of consumers' narrative transportation. *Journal of Consumer Research*, 40(5), 797–817.

Vila, O.M. and Bharadwaj, S. (2017). Competing on social purpose. *Harvard Business Review*. Available at: https://hbr.org/2017/09/competing-on-social-purpose.

Weick, K.E. and Robertsm, K.H. (1993). Collective mind in organizations: Heedful interrelating on flight decks. *Administrative Science Quarterly*, 38(3), 357–381.

2. Becton Dickinson & Co (BD): *Advancing the World of Health*

INTRODUCTION

Two medical salesmen, Maxwell W. Becton and Fairleigh S. Dickinson, met by chance at a train station. They shared a common vision to improve the lives of their customers. Their friendship and shared vision led to them setting up Becton Dickinson in 1897 in Franklin Lakes, New Jersey, to sell medical thermometers and syringes.

In the subsequent decades, BD, as the company is known today, saw exponential growth in terms of product offerings, technology advancement, international offices and manufacturing facilities across the globe. Today, BD is known across the world as a global medical technology company with a purpose anchored in "Advancing the World of Health". The company is focused on providing innovative solutions that help to advance medical research and genomics, enhance the diagnosis of infectious disease and cancer, improve medication management, promote infection prevention, equipping surgical and interventional procedures and supporting the management of diabetes.

Occasionally, purpose emerges from within organizations when managers spot and then champion opportunities for social innovation. At BD, a key highlight was the development of the world's first safety-engineered syringe in 1988. This syringe helped to reduce the incidence of HIV and other needle-based infections among healthcare workers as a result of needle stick injuries. Over time, its efforts in developing similar products to advance the world of health coalesced into the purpose statement that now defines the company.

BD offers a wide range of capabilities that help healthcare providers advance the world of health by improving medical discovery, diagnostics and the delivery of care. Be it a lab researcher or a nurse handling hazardous drugs or a physician prescribing medication, BD has capabilities that can enhance healthcare outcomes, lower costs, increase efficiencies, improve safety and expand access to healthcare ecosystems around the world.

ARTICULATE

A top-down approach does not work when trying to get employees to believe in a company's purpose, values and culture, according to James Lim, President of BD for Greater Asia. To demonstrate this, Mr Lim cited a proposed meeting in 2013 at BD's headquarters in New Jersey, where BD's new global CEO intended to gather the company's top 300 global leaders to articulate the company's new purpose, values and culture. The CEO wanted this information to be disseminated down globally. However, Mr. Lim felt that more effective engagement needed to be done on the ground, and was not shy to tell the global CEO his views:

> "It's not going to achieve your goal. You reach 300 people; how do you know that those 300 will reach 35,000 people worldwide? How do you ensure that our leaders commit to cascade their story down to the last person in the organization with the same clarity and inspiration. If you want to get engagement, some of our global executive leadership team should fly to every region,

and I will work with global and regional management on activities to engage associates on the ground together".

The global CEO listened to Mr. Lim, and subsequently visited Asia with four of his associates from the BD executive leadership team. Lim managed to get all Greater Asia Pacific leaders to stand up and articulate the purpose, values and culture alongside the global leadership team. According to Lim:

> "It is only when people have 'skin in the game' that a company can truly live its purpose. If it is someone sitting down and just listening to the message from HQ, he/she cannot create example stories that are localized to inspire associates".

To allow employees to reach their full potential, the articulation of a company's vision is not sufficient. Mr. Lim also places a great importance on the motto "to foster learning, emphasize doing". He elaborated that the best way to foster sustained learning does not come from hearing somebody, reading from textbooks or articles or attending courses. Instead, it emerges through the identification and undertaking of pivotal experiences that mould and shape the life of an individual. When an individual has amassed considerable diverse experiences, he or she will be a leader that is able to gain the trust and leadership of bosses, peers and subordinates. Mr Lim also believes that such holistic experiences will allow one to live, articulate and execute BD's purpose, and lead others in a genuine way.

BD makes a presence at various events to communicate the impact that the company makes on health issues worldwide. Participating in such events gives BD leaders a unique opportunity to make a strong and lasting impression while introducing new product innovations, demonstrating products, providing education and sharing success stories.

Lim describes the company's purpose as a "North Star":

"Every decision that an individual makes should fulfil our purpose while achieving win–win outcomes for both the customer (e.g. hospitals) and the patient. When demand exceeds supply, we are faced with an ethical dilemma: Do we sell to the highest bidder to maximize profit, or do we fulfil the needs of existing customers (Hospitals and Governments) with more urgent medical needs and not base only on propensity to pay"? There is definitely an economic benefit to our P&L, but there is also a humane need to step up and deliver. It is at times like this that our purpose guides us like the North Star".

Since BD has a clearly articulated purpose that is ingrained into its DNA, decision-making when dealing with dilemmas like this can be easily reconciled. When faced with a global pandemic, BD's purpose directs the people at the company to support governments and hospitals with the required diagnostic tools where they are needed the most; P&L is not the only focus at times like these, it is **advancing the world of health.**

ASSIMILATE

BD makes it part of its recruiting process to get new employees to align their individual purpose with the company's corporate purpose. In addition to looking at competencies and fit for the job, BD's recruiters articulate the company's purpose very explicitly to the candidates and examine if the new recruits' aspirations and values can complement the purpose of the organization. While this may be a tedious procedure to follow, this emphasis on purpose has helped BD to attract talented individuals who have a passion towards our philanthropy, corporate social responsibility and shared values. These include people who are driven to work in the healthcare space, perhaps because of the loss of a loved one due to the lack of proper medical care, or because they have had someone in the family with a medical issue or needs. BD has been able to channel these people to work in specific departments where their passion for finding solutions can be nurtured and fulfilled.

Of course, BD finds itself fortunate to be in an industry where corporate purpose is seamlessly aligned with what individuals aspire to do, in other words, the ability to "do your life's work in your work life". As healthcare is a very noble cause, it is common for people who join BD to bring with them the values of servant leadership. At the start of the COVID-19 pandemic in Asia, BD had to install medical instruments in various treatment centers requiring urgent setup. Said Lim:

> "It was heartening to witness the number of volunteers who put up their hands to step up and serve their country during this time of need. This is at a time when a healthy person would prefer to stay away from a hospital or be anywhere close to where there is a possibility of contracting infection. One story that resonates with me was during the beginning of the COVID-19 pandemic in Wuhan, an individual from BD China based in Shanghai volunteered to install a diagnostic instrument in urgent need for testing in the epicentre in Wuhan. This person traveled from Shanghai to Wuhan (1000 km) with the help of a fellow colleague who drove him to the outskirts of the city. There they were met by two BD Technicians from Wuhan who helped navigate all the hurdles as the city was being locked down by authorities. He managed to install the instrument and had to stay back in Wuhan to be quarantined for two weeks. This commitment to customer, patient and healthcare workers comes from living the purpose. So, when values and purpose are aligned, ordinary people will go out of the way to do extraordinary things".

Along with the prevailing law of the land, each BD leader and employee is expected to follow an ethical framework. As the company undergoes changes in senior leadership again in 2020, this is one endearing aspect that remains rooted within every BD leader: standards of behavior that focus on five values. These are:

(1) doing what is right,
(2) thriving on innovation and quality,
(3) being accountable,
(4) learning and improving every day and
(5) helping each other be great.

Doing what is right is the cornerstone of BD's Code. To do what is right, each BD employee is expected to follow the rule of law, rules and company policies that apply to them in the region they operate. In addition, each person is expected to follow the highest ethical standards, even when there is no specific law or policy. The BD Code provides guidance, especially when employees face a dilemma on the right course of action. When decisions are made based on these values, BD's ethical culture is strengthened, risk is minimized and the company's reputation is protected. You can change culture by constant re-enforcing of the right ethical behaviors.

As aptly described by BD's former CEO, Vince Forlenza:

"With unwavering commitment to our culture and values, we follow the simple principle: We do what is right". This guides every decision we make, every action we take and every interaction we have — with our customers, our business partners, our communities and each other. This also includes speaking up when we have concerns and seeking help when we have questions. Just as I base my behavior on our cultural priorities and the Code's guidance, we expect everyone at BD to do the same. Nothing is more essential for our success and for fulfilling our purpose and potential at BD".

BD's Greater Asia leaders also use storytelling to embed purpose into the company's cultural fabric. More specifically, they use stories to bring alive challenges, possibilities and solutions in their day-to-day interactions with employees. Storytelling invokes emotions, engages the listener and inspires questions, comments and interaction. BD's provision of support and relief packages during natural disasters in Greater Asia offers BD leaders a rich repository of real incidents and stories that can be shared internally to demonstrate purpose in action. According to Lim, "Storytelling helps us to be more persuasive, compelling, relatable and etches a permanent mark in the minds of the listener".

BD also facilitates the assimilation of purpose through workspace design. For example, following its acquisition of new companies (e.g. Bard and CareFusion), BD ensures that new offices are redesigned to create collaborative workspaces that promote greater levels of cohesion and engagement across existing and new team members.

ACTIVATE

What a purpose-driven organization like BD can elicit from its people is a different level of engagement and contribution towards building "shared value", which aims to achieve both goals of increasing revenues and creating positive social impact. Since 2004, BD Global Health has championed private sector engagement with international agencies, nongovernmental organizations and governments on global, regional and local levels — with the goal of enhancing access to health for all people. BD also works with external funders and scientific collaborators to incubate global health technologies that address unmet needs in emerging nations.

Governments and non-government organizations are important stakeholders and partners for BD. The company has established numerous public–private partnerships (PPPs) to address unmet health needs in developing countries. For example, it was BD's PPP with the World Health Organization (WHO) and the Bill & Melinda Gates Foundation that resulted in the creation of the BD Odon device — a low-cost tool designed to assist vaginal birth that is currently in clinical trials. In cases of prolonged or complicated labor, doctors are often required to use tools such as forceps in the second stage of labor. Such tools and skills for assisted vaginal birth, however, are too often not available, especially in remote areas, leading to mothers being rushed to referral hospitals for a cesarean section. This delay and complications in this second stage of labor sometimes lead to maternal and neonatal morbidity and mortality. However, the BD Odon device can facilitate vaginal delivery in prolonged or complicated labor by reducing contact between the baby's skull and the birth canal. This easy-to-use device has the potential to significantly reduce maternal and neonatal deaths worldwide. BD has agreed to manufacture and distribute the device, and has estimated that it could be created at an affordable and cost-effective price point. BD Odon is expected to be used by midwives as well as obstetricians who would need minimal training to use the device effectively. The WHO has given favorable reviews on the device and has recognized its "potential to save the lives of mothers and newborns at the time of birth". It is an example of corporate purpose rallying multiple stakeholders to leverage on their respective strengths to create shared value and solve a serious problem.

Another purpose-driven initiative that BD has been pursuing in the region is a multi-faceted initiative against Anti-Microbial Resistance (AMR). Anti-microbials are drugs that kill infectious bacteria, viruses, parasites and fungi. The limited development of new medicines and decades of antibiotics misuse have driven an increase in the number of microbes that are resistant to these lifesaving drugs.

BD's efforts are ongoing in this area, but they already offer a broad portfolio of AMR solutions that support infection prevention and control, diagnostic testing and surveillance and reporting. In 2019, BD's work on AMR was highlighted by *Fortune* magazine.

BD has also supported international agencies in their quest to eradicate polio. In 2018, BD donated 20 million syringes valued at US$1 million to a non-profit organization dedicated to tackling the world's most pressing humanitarian challenges, including the eradication of polio. These 20 million syringes were distributed among four states in India — Maharashtra, West Bengal, Tamil Nadu and Haryana. In 1954, the company made similar contributions to the first polio eradication efforts in the US.

The ongoing COVID-19 crisis has acutely highlighted the need to strengthen infection prevention, diagnostics and surveillance in the region. BD stepped in to address these areas by helping to identify patients at greatest risk of acquiring infections, monitor population-based trends and provide early warning for outbreaks. The support BD provides to healthcare systems in Asia will eventually become central to their strategy and a sure way to activate their purpose to advance the world of health.

Like all private companies, BD needs to closely monitor its profitability. However, Lim emphasized that the performance and reputation of the company do not solely lie in P&L. Instead, he believes that the creation of shared value is critical to protecting a company's license to operate and its long-term sustainability. Furthermore, the need to engage the hearts and souls of BD's associates makes the activation of purpose to create shared value an imperative. For helping to make the world a better place, *Fortune* magazine named BD three times in the last five years in its "Change the World" list.

CONCLUSION

The pursuit of a purpose-driven strategy and shared value opportunities has enabled BD to "advance the world of health". Acting with integrity has always been the cornerstone of BD, is recognized as critical to the company's success and reputation and is crucial to achieving alignment with the company's purpose. BD's commitment extends beyond compliance with the law. The company has emphasized that the best way to be a great company and to deliver value to their customers, associates and shareholders is to be fair, honest and ethical in their business practices when dealing with external stakeholders in the community they serve. All BD employees are encouraged to speak up and report actual or suspected violations of laws, the Code, BD policies or relevant industry codes. BD has clearly assimilated this purpose among its stakeholders by publicizing this internally and externally. These efforts have proven to the world that establishing a purpose-oriented culture will enable the company to leverage and harness the best from its associates.

3. DBS Bank Ltd (DBS):
Making Banking Joyful

INTRODUCTION

At independence in 1965, Singapore was an undeveloped country with no natural resources. Its main advantage was its strategic location as a shipping port for trade. The Singapore government's early development goal was to ensure economic growth. This was to be accomplished by executing a plan to industrialize and to develop export-oriented industries. The Development Bank of Singapore[1] was formed in 1968 to facilitate financing for this effort.

In 1998, DBS merged with Post Office Savings Bank (POSB), a local bank that was key in promoting thrift and savings among Singaporeans. Whereas DBS was thought of by Singaporeans as the 'national' development bank, POSB was the first national savings bank for the mass market in Singapore.

Since the acquisition, DBS has had a leading position in Singapore in its three lines of businesses — consumer banking and wealth management, institutional banking and global financial markets. The bank has a strong Asian presence, particularly in Singapore and Hong Kong. In 2012, DBS re-articulated its purpose as **"Make Banking Joyful"**, which ushered in an era of cultural and digital transformation.

---

[1] It changed its name to DBS Bank in 2003 to reflect its growing international presence.

ARTICULATE

Purpose is integral to DBS' DNA. The bank was "established as part of a series of institutional reforms designed to meet the changing requirements of the Singapore economy" (1968 DBS Annual Report). Specifically, its role as a development bank was to help spur the development of industry in a fledging Singapore. From the early days, its guiding ethos was always "if it is good for the country, then it is the right thing for us to do". At that time, the bank financed nascent industries — including taking equity stakes in companies — to encourage foreign investments that were key to the creation of jobs then. It also undertook the development of several ground-breaking projects, including building the nation's first shopping mall as well as convention centre. All these proved to be a catalyst for Singapore's economic development during the country's formative years.

However, in the 50 years since DBS' founding, banking has been fundamentally redefined by the digital revolution. With the ubiquity of the smartphone, the explosion of data and the rise of the sharing economy, customer behaviours are dramatically different now from what they were before – customers now expect a new kind of banking. Bill Gates once famously said: "People don't need banks, they need banking". This led to soul searching that prompted the bank to question the very purpose of banking itself. Studies have shown that few people enjoy carrying out their banking activities.

Sim S. Lim, DBS Group Executive, Consumer Banking/Wealth Management elaborates:

> *"Banks were very archaic and mundane. The language for you to sign was so difficult to understand. It was 'our way or the highway'. Fintech came and showed that banks are slow, banks are*

bureaucratic, and that people didn't even understand the terms and conditions. Our team woke up and said, fintech is going to take away our lunch if we don't change. Ironically, Fintech is the best thing to happen to the banking industry these past 10 years".

DBS saw the challenge as an opportunity to reimagine banking in the new disruptive landscape. According to Lim, the bank changed from having a company-centric mindset that focused on what was best for the bank to a customer-focused one that asks the question: "If we were the customers, what would we want? How can we understand what we are signing? How is the customers' journey"? This change in the mindset started DBS' customer-led journey.

Under the leadership of DBS CEO Piyush Gupta and his senior leadership team, DBS re-articulated its purpose as "Making Banking Joyful", as Singapore has already developed into a high-income country. As Gupta said in a media interview:

"Almost three-fourths of the world would rather go to the dentist than to a bank. If DBS is successful in making it less of a painful chore, then we think we can create a very different kind of bank, one that is a joy to bank with".[2]

Three focal areas are embedded into this new purpose: First, make banking so simple and hassle-free that customers have more time to spend on the people or things they care about. In Lim's words:

"We want to make banking invisible, whereby you're using us every day without realizing that you're using us. That's when we

---

[2] https://www.forbes.com/sites/jonathansalembaskin/2015/12/21/can-dbs-make-banking-joyful/#2fdb9ebf9888

have really seeped into your lives and into your everyday needs without you realizing that we're part of your lives and your everyday journey".

Second, enable customers — individuals or businesses — to seize life's opportunities. Third, create platforms and opportunities so customers and partners can live larger than themselves. Externally, the new purpose is expressed as the "Live More, Bank Less" brand promise and campaign. Implicit in the message is the promise that customers who bank with DBS will have their banking chores taken care of easily and quickly, so that they can get on with their lives.

ASSIMILATE

Because of its heritage, embedding purpose into the culture and social fabric of DBS has been less of a challenge for the bank than for other organizations. As Gupta explained:

"It's enshrined in our roots. You go back to DBS' formation. DBS was created by the Singapore Economic Development Board to help in the development and growth of Singapore. The people who have been around the past 40 years [and those that came after them] have that sense of mission. We were created to help Singapore grow. Our job was not to make money. Our job was to help create and make something better for this country. And it became clear to me that this whole sense of 'we're bigger than just shareholder, profit or shareholder value' is deeply ingrained in the psyche of our people. So, for us, making sure that having a clear understanding of what is our purpose going forward, and making sure it's deeply embedded in the company, is not as challenging as it is for many other companies".

Internally, this purpose is enshrined as one of DBS' corporate values, which are represented by the acronym PRIDE!:

Purpose-driven: creating impact beyond banking;
Relationship-led: building long-lasting relationships and teams;
Innovative: embracing change to add value;
Decisive: our people have the freedom to think, act and own;
Everything Fun!: Everything Fun! We believe in having fun and celebrating successes together.

According to Lim, this set of values allows people to say what the company stands for (or does not stand for). It also establishes what are the commonly acceptable practices or behaviours so that people do not need to ask "Can I do this"? or "Can I do that"?

The PRIDE values are shared with new employees, cascaded through townhalls and internal forums, and lived out in the day-to-day with leaders expected to model the right behaviours. Employees are annually appraised not just on their business achievements but also on whether they have exemplified the PRIDE! values.

For Gupta, the key is to translate purpose into behaviours:

"That is the work we need to do: Define for people with a degree of clarity what good behavior means, and what behaviors we don't like in this company. If you get that right, there can also be a rubric for improvement. So when you hire people, you know what kind of people we want, people who strive to a certain set of behaviors, and not people who don't. We can use that to determine and define how we build leadership. And if you can do that, then you can really have a whole agenda around customer- centricity, change etc. – driven by the soul of what DBS needs to be".[3]

---

[3] Chong, M. (2014). DBS: Transforming the culture of an Asian bank. The Case Centre.

Nonetheless, the assimilation of "making banking joyful" into the culture of DBS happened against the backdrop of its transformation from a conservative regulated bank to a '26,000-person startup' (starting in 2014). To do that, DBS looked to global technology giants such as Google, Amazon and Netflix for inspiration and set about building a startup culture. It set up an innovation team to foster a culture of innovation across the organization. It defined five desired staff behavioral traits: 1) Agile, 2) customer obsessed, 3) data driven, 4) take risk and experiment, and 5) be a learning organization.

It identified blockers to change and introduced enablers to change, including redesigning offices spaces to foster collaboration. It conducted over 1,000 experiments involving more than 17,000 employees and set KPIs around them. It partnered its employees with startups, fintechs, other companies and universities in hackathons, which exposed them to new ways of doing business and bridged the digital divide between senior and junior bankers. These hackathons gave the bank a plethora of ideas to embed technology into banking. Perhaps the most notable outcome of the hackathons is the creation of Digibank in India – an entirely mobile-centric banking service with no brick-and-mortar branches. As Digibank leverages AI-driven automation, it can scale quickly across Asia to make banking 'joyful' for millions of customers. Last but not least, DBS transformed its training programs to create opportunities for learning by doing. In addition, it has invested S$20 million over five years to groom its 10,000 Singapore-based employees to embrace new technologies.

DBS' 'Four Quadrants' framework has also been pivotal to educating and empowering its staff on how to 'make banking joyful' for its customers. The four elements of the framework are:

1. Augmented banking: It is about enhancing the customer's relationship with the bank by delivering an enriched experienced both in terms of new and existing services with new ways of

interaction. DBS' response to augmented banking is the digitization of the entire bank.

2. Open banking: It is about combining services from other suppliers with those of the bank to offer enhanced value to the customer over individual offerings. Internally, DBS refers to this as the "rise of the eco-systems".

3. Cognitive banking: It is about integrating and analyzing relevant data to present the customer with unique tailored recommendations. This translates into a quest to be the "intelligent bank" and to hyper-personalize offerings for all customers.

4. Automation banking: It is about pairing intelligent automation with the bank's resources to align the way employees work with the new customer journey. DBS now designs for 'no operations', 'no branches' and 'no cash' when introducing new products.

Lim gives an example of how the framework might work in practice:

> *"If you are a credit card manager, by letting people apply for a card using the app, you are using the augmented part of the quadrant. By working with the telco partner to reach 100,000 customers, that's the ecosystem part. By enabling a credit card application to go through and issuing the card to the customer within a day, that's automation banking. By understanding the data that we have on the customer, that he is good for $10,000 a month, the credit limit, that is cognitive banking. So, the product manager has all these quadrants of banking without realizing that he's using it".*

In 2016, DBS launched an online mini-series titled *Sparks* that follows a group of young bankers as they navigate their work and personal lives. The mini-series is inspired by true stories of social enterprises and their journeys. For example, the first three episodes are based on the story of clean energy firm Sunseap Leasing, which

DBS helped to finance at a time when clean energy financing was not a norm in the country. Through *Sparks*, DBS aims to challenge the perception that banking is only about transactions. The first season of Sparks has garnered more than 250 million views. In June 2019, DBS debuted the show's second season, which explores social issues including plastic pollution, food waste and social inequality.

Branded content such as *Sparks* can help articulate a company's purpose to its internal and external stakeholders and facilitate its assimilation. Said Karen Ngui, Managing Director and Head of Group Strategic Marketing & Communications:

> *"As much as people see the numbers, dollars and cents behind every client, there is always a deeper story to tell. What makes Sparks different is it shows the challenges the characters face in the bank. While they have good and bad days, when they see how their work makes a difference to the lives of their clients, that is very rewarding".*[4]

---

[4] https://www.marketing-interactive.com/dbs-hopes-new-mini-series-will-challenge-perception-banking

ACTIVATE

DBS' purpose of "Making Banking Joyful" is activated largely through financial action. In support of its financial inclusion agenda, DBS offers social enterprises in Singapore unsecured business loans at a preferential rate of 5% fixed per annum. In 2018, the DBS Foundation awarded S$1.25 million in grants to 12 social enterprises. The grants enable social enterprises to develop prototypes of their ideas, add critical capabilities for business sustainability, or scale up existing businesses. In the same year, DBS employees mentored more than 50 social enterprises across its six core markets to help scale their businesses. Said Gupta:

> *"While there may indeed be some trade-offs between maximising shareholder returns and providing societal benefits in the short term, ensuring productive outcomes for society is completely consistent with the interests of the shareholder in the long term. The reason for this is quite simple: while businesses often need regulatory licences to operate, what is easily forgotten is that they need another licence as well — a social licence. This social licence is critical, because if society or the citizenry does not see any value in a business' existence, it is doomed to extinction. The only way to have a long-term sustainable business is to ensure that society's expectations are met. While regulatory licences can be applied for, such social licences — like respect — must be earned".*

COVID-19 Response

The purpose of DBS was brought into sharp relief during the COVID-19 pandemic. It rolled out a variety of measures across a number of Asian countries to make banking less onerous for its stakeholders. In Singapore, for example, its consumer banking division granted a six-month moratorium for principal repayment on mortgages. In addition, it offered a free 30-day COVID-19 relief insurance coverage in partnership with Chubb Insurance Singapore that attracted more than one million customers and their family members.

The bank was also well equipped for the significant increase in demand for digital banking services during the pandemic. In March 2020, it launched a digital relief package to help its food and beverage clients set up online operations in just three business days. With the help of two Singapore-based tech start-ups, Oddle and FirstCom, DBS helped its food and beverage clients to establish an online presence through e-menus, digital shopfronts and social media presence. In April 2020, its POSB subsidiary supplemented these efforts by opening about 41,000 bank accounts for migrant workers (a figure that is triple the usual monthly sign-up rate for this group). This initiative allowed migrant workers who were quarantined in dormitories to gain access to digital banking services via the POSB Jolly app.[5]

Its institutional banking division granted a six-month and nine-month repayment moratorium respectively for existing commercial and refinanced commercial property loans. Other notable measures include the extension of import facilities of up to 60 days to help SMEs cope with supply chain disruptions as well as the introduction of a collateral-free digital business loan.

DBS extended several of the same offers to customers in India, Hong Kong and Taiwan. DBS is not the major bank in those countries, so customers there were very surprised that a Singaporean Bank would go out of the way to do this for them.

---

[5] Ang, P. (2020. Sep 6). DBS named world's best bank in nod to its response to Covid-19. The Straits Times. Available at: https://www.straitstimes.com/business/banking/dbs-named-best-bank-in-the-world-in-nod-to-its-response-to-covid-19-crisis

Despite its recent pivot to "making banking joyful", DBS' founding purpose of financing Singapore's economic growth remains very much alive. During the COVID-19 pandemic, the company pledged to hire more than 2,000 people in Singapore in 2020. More than 1,000 of these roles are apprenticeships for fresh graduates and more specialized jobs for experienced professionals. According to Gupta:

> "It seemed right to us to not just continue with hiring for business-as-usual activities, but also to actively create new jobs where we can, so as to help more people tide through this difficult period. In particular, we want to do our part to avoid having a 'lost' generation of young graduates in Singapore whose career prospects are jeopardised because they are unable to find jobs due to the pandemic".[6]

DBS also gave an assurance to its 12,000-strong Singapore workforce that there would be no job cuts. Moreover, all employees remained on full pay. This happened at a time when numerous other firms were cutting salaries and retrenching or furloughing staff.

While the purpose of "making banking joyful" has taken precedence in recent years, the company's actions during the pandemic show that its original purpose never went away.

CONCLUSION

The DBS story shows the dynamic nature of corporate purpose. Having fulfilled its initial purpose of supporting Singapore's early industrialization, DBS went on to re-articulate it (i.e. "Making

---

[6] https://www.todayonline.com/singapore/dbs-hire-more-2000-people-singapore-despite-covid-19-economic-slowdown

Banking Joyful") to remain relevant in the digital age. It is remarkable that in less than 10 years, Gupta and his senior leadership team have succeeded in transforming the bank by getting everyone to 'sing from the same hymn book'. This is a story where purpose originated from the top and ultimately got accepted by the employees.

The bank's success in articulating, assimilating and activating its purpose has resulted in global recognition:

GLOBAL BANK OF THE YEAR	BEST BANK IN THE WORLD	WORLD'S BEST DIGITAL BANK	GLOBAL SME BANK OF THE YEAR	BEST SERVICE CASH MANAGEMENT NON-FI - OVERALL	BEST PRIVATE BANK FOR INNOVATION
The Banker	Global Finance	Euromoney	Global SME Finance (Managed by International Finance Corporation)	Euromoney Cash Management Survey	PWM & The Banker

In addition, it won the Euromoney "World's Best Bank" award in 2020. With this win, DBS became the first bank in the world to hold three of the global best bank awards concurrently. However, it is the company's activation of its purpose — both old and new — during the COVID-19 crisis that may come to define its legacy.

4. Kova Paints Group (Kova): Providing Vietnamese People with Sustainable and Affordable Living Environments

KOVA PAINT

Kova Paint was founded in 1993 by chemist Professor Nguyen Thi Hoe, who is affectionately called "Professor" throughout the company. In the 25 years since then, Kova has grown into one of the largest paint companies in Vietnam, employing about 1000 employees in several countries, and operating six factories in Vietnam itself. The company has seven representative offices and more than 1000 retailers. Despite its very humble beginnings, Professor Hoe and her team have been able to transform Kova into a company and brand that matter to customers, employees and many other stakeholders, by **providing Vietnamese people with sustainable and affordable living environments through science-based products.**

ARTICULATE

Born into a poor family in Nghe An province in central Vietnam, Professor Hoe began her scientific training in the midst of the Vietnam conflict with the United States in the 1960s. To pay for her education and support her young family during a time of war and food shortages, she raised pigs while in school. After graduation, she joined the faculty at Hanoi University of Technology and later at the University of Can Tho. It was during these teaching years that her dream of doing something that bears her own stamp was born.

In the 1970s, Vietnam had just been unified. As a poor country, the Vietnamese people's common wish was to earn enough money to put food on the table for themselves and their families. In addition to having three square meals a day, Professor Hoe believed they deserved to live in beautiful, affordable and safe homes.

At that time, however, paint was mostly imported, costly and not suited to Vietnam's hot and humid climate. So, Professor Hoe came up with the idea of developing a paint product using local, cheaper materials that could address the demands of Vietnam's climate. In her endeavors, she was driven by the belief that scientists like her have a moral obligation to use their knowledge to make a positive social and economic impact through the products they develop.

In the late 1980s, Professor Hoe discovered a method for water-proofing paint, a process that could help people protect their homes against humidity and the wet climate. For her achievement in waterproofing research, Professor Hoe was invited to the US in 1992 to receive the Kovalevskaya Award — a prize awarded to women with scientific research projects that served their country and society. During the trip, she established a partnership with a Californian company to localize paint formulas for each region — with its own unique climatic conditions — in Vietnam. To this day, "tropicalization" exemplifies KOVA's purpose of providing Vietnamese people with sustainable and affordable living environments through science-based products.

Professor Hoe officially founded the Kova Group in 1993, coining the name of her company from the name of the Kovalevskaya award. At the start, she ran her company from a small laboratory in the Ho Chi

Minh University of Technology as a family-run business. Most of her team at that time comprised family members and scientists who shared her vision. However, during the first three years, the company incurred heavy losses, as the executive board was inexperienced and production costs were very high. Many members in Kova's senior management wanted to give up, but she persevered.

Professor Hoe's perseverance ultimately paid off, as Kova's paint eventually gained popularity not only in Vietnam but also in neighbouring countries such as Singapore, Indonesia, Malaysia, Laos and Cambodia. The company's internationalization was driven by its mission of promoting Vietnamese technology — and bringing the benefits of this technology — beyond Vietnam to the rest of the world. While many Vietnamese brands aspire to mimic foreign brands, Kova aspires to do just the opposite — that is, "to bring the pride of Vietnamese technology to the rest of the world".

Professor Hoe has succeeded in articulating Kova's purpose through her own lifelong devotion to it — she leads by "walking the walk". Now in her seventies, she still works an average of 14 hours per day in her labs. Her purpose-driven story has proven to be an inspiration to Kova staff such as Thien Ly Nguyen Truong, Marketing Director of KOVA Trading:

> "Professor Hoe is a rare case of achieving her extraordinary success in commercializing her scientific researches in Vietnam and going global. Having engaged with Professor Hoe for more than 5 years, there are more reasons for me, as an employee, to believe that her journey and legacy at Kova are absolutely not about luck. There have been stories being told from generation to generation for the past 25 years on how we should be proud to be part of KOVA's family. However, there is no powerful story than witnessing her as a Chairwoman, arriving to the office in the early morning and only back home very late. At her age,

every single day, spending non-stop working hours in the lab and independently traveling to conferences, projects, meetings, from big to small, just to ensure that people out there get the finest product for their home as they could ever ask for. A scientist not only gives you inventions, they're actually giving you a belief that everything is possible, no matter where we come from".

ASSIMILATE

Kova's purpose of helping Vietnamese people to have better homes and live better lives is embedded into its business strategy and culture. First, the company has a Sustainable Development Strategy that fosters a single-minded focus on the development of paint products that are environmentally friendly, non-toxic and water-based. In line with this strategy, Kova does not operate in the marine coating sector, as the anti-fouling properties of marine paints require a certain degree of toxicity. Kova is also committed to producing only 100% water-based, environmentally friendly products.

Second, Kova has created a company culture where employees embody its purpose. It is an environment in which employees feel engaged in producing innovations that make their communities and the world better, thus becoming a force for change. Kova has done so through the strategies of "informing", "motivating" and "developing capabilities":

> **Informing:** Kova's senior management strongly believes there is a deep relationship between core beliefs and values on the one hand, and employee pride, performance and retention on the other. Each month, Nguyen Duy, CEO of Kova Trading (and Professor Hoe's grandson), gathers the employees together to reiterate Kova's purpose and pride in being one of the outstanding science-driven enterprises in Vietnam. The gathering also gives employees the opportunity to share their stories.

In 2018, Kova conducted the first of its annual employee surveys to assess how well employees understand Kova's mission, vision, core values and business goals. With these insights, Nguyen Duy and the internal communication team plan to more deeply embed Kova's purpose into employees' behavior and fine-tune Kova's internal messaging.

Motivating: Motivation at Kova comes less through rewards than through the personal satisfaction employees derive from their participation in social initiatives. Each year, 80% of Kova employees collectively volunteer thousands of hours to support the Kova Prize and the Kova-founded Startup Vietnam Foundation (more on both in the following section). Having said that, CEO Nguyen Duy is mindful that more can be done through HR policy and internal communication to motivate and reward desired employee behavior.

Developing capabilities: All Kova employees undergo orientation in their first few days to familiarize them with Kova's organizational culture. The orientation includes three sessions that introduce employees to the company's structure, policy and rules; corporate values and culture; and internal processes. New senior managers are guided directly by CEO Nguyen Duy or by other members of the Board of Directors.

ACTIVATE

Kova belongs to a class of purpose-driven companies (like the others featured in this book) that have built a reputation for social impact among its external stakeholders. To amplify its purpose beyond the company, Kova set up the Kova Prize and the Startup Vietnam Foundation (SVF). As a reflection of their importance, Kova allocates about 10% of its annual profits to these two social projects.

Advocacy through the Kova Prize

Professor Hoe launched the Kova Prize in 2002, as she wasn't content with inspiring just Kova employees — she wanted the purpose to inspire others beyond the walls of the company. Through the Kova Prize, she aims to:

1. Encourage applied scientific research.
2. Recognize humanitarian activities.
3. Nurture young scientific talent in Vietnam.
4. Support excellent students who have challenging family conditions.

It has helped Kova to build a positive nationwide reputation that attracts young, talented Vietnamese associates who are inspired by the company's purpose. The competition associated with the prize also offers Kova employees a visceral platform to activate and contribute to this purpose — for example, hundreds of Kova employees get the opportunity to mentor the young participants, even long after the event is over. In addition to giving the prize money, Kova takes care of all of the participants' expenses related to food, transport and lodging for the participants and their parents.

Innovating and driving strategic partnerships through Startup Vietnam Foundation

Nguyen Duy founded Startup Vietnam Foundation in 2014 to support the country's emerging startup ecosystem by providing entrepreneurs with leadership training, technology consulting, investor connections and product commercialization in both domestic and international markets. Duy explains the rationale for SVF:

> "We want to be a role model. We're building an infrastructure where people can learn about leadership, talk to mentors and find partners in HR, finance, accounting, legal, marketing and technology. We are building a platform to enable them to connect with various stakeholders and resources in the startup ecosystem. We have about 100 mentors, a lot of investors and business enterprises, which are all willing to support startups. We have connections with the National Academy of Technology, so we have access to more than 3,000 scientists, and every year we receive a fund from the government. We've also promoted the globalization story to these startups and helped them take their products out of the Vietnam market".

Like the Kova Prize, SVF activates and amplifies Kova's purpose by empowering tech entrepreneurs to create solutions with positive social and economic impact for Vietnam. It has done so by acting as a platform that connects entrepreneurs with key stakeholders and resources in the startup ecosystem. While the SVF is driven by an altruistic purpose, it has also benefited Kova in a significant way:

> "The value we gain is much higher than what we give. Because what we gain is the trust from society. If we're talking about the business case, then it is this: We don't have to spend too much money to gain the trust of the end-consumer. In addition, when we work with the startup founders, all the inside knowledge we get while working with them is helping us in the way we work

daily. It enlightens the way we look at things and the way we solve them. It makes us more innovative".

To date, SVF has established partnerships with more than 30 international startup organizations funded by ASEAN, Korean, Indian, Swedish, Australian, Polish, Canadian and other governments.

CONCLUSION

Professor Hoe started her enterprise with a burning sense of purpose — to enable Vietnamese to live in homes with beautiful, affordable and safe paints on their walls. She single-mindedly articulated that purpose by harnessing her scientific knowledge to develop paint products with cheaper local materials that protect homes in Vietnam's humid climate. Once she officially established Kova, she and her team assimilated that purpose into the cultural fabric of the company through informing, motivating and developing employee capabilities. Finally, Kova activates its purpose by engaging external stakeholders through the Kova Prize and Startup Vietnam Foundation. These initiatives in turn generate positive word-of-mouth publicity that amplifies Kova's purpose-driven story throughout Vietnam.

Kova is still a relatively young company that needs to more systematically embed its purpose into its organizational culture, particularly through recognition, training and internal communication. But it is already an excellent example of what "good looks like" in a developing Asian country.

5. LIXIL Group Corp (LIXIL): *Making Better Homes a Reality for Everyone, Everywhere*[1]

INTRODUCTION

Post-merger integration (PMI) is hard. Studies indicate that as many as one in every two PMI efforts fares poorly. There are many factors that come into play, including operational issues, relevant expertise and the complexity of synergies. Many corporate leaders will acknowledge that the "soft factors", such as employee motivation, can be equally or more important than the "hard factors". But getting a grasp of these "soft" issues and figuring out a clear plan that will engage and motivate employees around a shared purpose is not easy and all too often falls down the list of priorities during PMI.

This was the challenge facing LIXIL in 2015. You may not have heard of LIXIL, but you will likely have heard of its brands. LIXIL is the corporation that was established when five leading companies in the Japanese housing and building products industry — Tostem, INAX, Shin Nikkei, SUNWAVE and Toyo Exteriors — were integrated in 2011. Following an initial period of integration in Japan, the company embarked on a rapid and ambitious global acquisition spree, acquiring brands including Permasteelisa, a global leader in curtain walls for major architectural projects such as the Shard in London

---

[1] Special thanks to John Short for contributing to this chapter.

and Apple's HQ campus in Cupertino, as well as leading water and sanitary ware brands including American Standard and GROHE.

Having established the company as a leader in its industry with more than 70,000 employees globally and operations in over 150 countries, the next stage of the company's evolution was to integrate and create a sense of "ONE LIXIL". But how do you do that with a company that is, on the one hand, brand new, but on the other hand, steeped in the history and culture embedded within the legacies of the companies that stretch back, in some cases, over 150 years? Management would often remark that the company had the feel of a 70,000 employee start-up with 100-year-old brands.

Regardless of whether employees became a part of LIXIL from INAX in Tokoname, GROHE in Dusseldorf, Cobra in Johannesburg, or American Standard in New Jersey, their feelings were the same. There was a strong sense of pride in the companies and brands that they had been a part of prior to integration, but there was very little as yet to provoke a real sense of shared pride in "being a part of LIXIL". What did LIXIL stand for? What was the shared vision that employees should be working towards, beyond simply profits? What was the company's bigger purpose?

So the need to articulate a clear and overarching purpose for the company primarily came not from pressures from the external operating environment, but from an internal urgency to align toward a "true North" and build a sense of pride and engagement in being LIXIL. This process culminated in the expression of LIXIL's purpose as "**making better homes a reality for everyone, everywhere**".

ARTICULATE

The process of articulating this new shared purpose combined both top-down and bottom-up activities. Back in 2015, management was setting out the vision in terms of the core business direction and financial goals, through initiatives such as the medium-term business strategy. In line with this process, the Public Affairs team began to interview and gather insights from the CEO and other executives on what it means to be LIXIL, what the company should stand for and where the company should be going.

At the same time, a cross-functional, bottom-up project was initiated to identify key areas of focus, targets and commitments. Pulling together insights from divisions such as R&D, Environment, Health & Safety, Marketing, Strategy, HR and Public Affairs, the team analyzed LIXIL's core areas of activity and expertise, and mapped this against best practices and white spaces within the sector. By doing this, we could understand where the company's purpose and contribution to society could bring high engagement internally and how LIXIL could truly differentiate itself from its peers. A full-day workshop was held with the cross-functional team to determine the key areas of focus, commitments and targets to really put meat against the bones of our LIXIL's purpose.

Through this process, and the reviews that followed within LIXIL's Corporate Responsibility Committee (CRC) and with management, we were able to articulate the direction through a newly formed Corporate Responsibility (CR) strategy and framework. This new framework built upon the company's core philosophy, which was that, "The Group's superior products and services contribute to improving people's comfort and lifestyles" and articulated clear focus areas where the company aimed to make a positive contribution.

The Corporate Responsibility strategy was founded on an overall commitment from LIXIL to make a positive impact in the communities in which we operate and on matters that require urgent action, leveraging our expertise, and covers three key strategic pillars:

1. Global Sanitation and Hygiene
   - An estimated two billion people — one out of every four in the world today — live without access to proper sanitation, of which approximately 670 million still defecate in the open on a daily basis. These are figures with a devastating human cost: 800 children under five years of age are estimated to die every day from diarrheal diseases caused by a lack of clean water and sanitary living conditions.
   - As a global leader in sanitary ware and water technology, LIXIL was in a unique position to be able to take its expertise in toilet design, development and marketing, and apply it to the global sanitation challenge. The company already had some nascent projects in this area, such as the SATO toilet, initially designed by a team of engineers at LIXIL's American Standard base in New Jersey with the support of the Bill & Melinda Gates Foundation, which was being used for cause-related marketing campaigns and donated primarily to partners in Bangladesh.
   - As opposed to other aspects of the CR strategy that may have been considered core commitments or "table stakes", sanitation and hygiene was identified as an initiative that was truly differentiated and uniquely LIXIL. Even within our industry, LIXIL was alone in being able to offer the full range of toilets, from the ultra-high-tech shower toilets that are so famed in Japan, right through to SATO and products that are specifically designed for emerging markets and rural off-grid applications where no proper sanitation infrastructure exists. If we could properly articulate and assimilate

this vision, it could become a powerful pillar in the purpose strategy, engaging stakeholders both inside and outside the company.

2. Water Conservation and Environmental Sustainability
   - Sustainable use of natural resources is ever more critical for our society, and given the nature of LIXIL's business, there are multiple areas where our actions can make a difference. By 2050, approximately four billion people (2 in 5) are expected to be living in areas of high water stress. Additionally, LIXIL's business is strongly linked to buildings, which account for 32% (24% residential and 8% commercial) of total global final energy use, and without action, energy use by buildings is estimated to more than double by 2050. With regards to other natural resources, aluminum, one of LIXIL's important raw materials, has been identified as one of the priority materials in the metals category and requires urgent attention.
   - LIXIL considers environmental challenges, such as water conservation and environmental protection, to be one of our most important business initiatives. As a company providing products and materials for living spaces, it was critical to demonstrate a commitment to our environmental strategy, which pledges that LIXIL will provide environmental solutions through our products and services.

3. Diversity and Inclusion
   - By 2050, more than one in every five people around the world are projected to be over the age of 60, with many living either alone or with their spouse only. Approximately 15% of the world's population today has some sort of disability, and this rate is increasing every year. In Japan, female participation in the workforce is still low compared to other countries, despite research suggesting that gender diversity correlates with less volatile and improved financial performance of corporations.

- As the third and final pillar of the CR strategy, LIXIL recognized its commitments to embracing the diversity of people in society and within our firm. This includes enhancing quality of life and well-being for the elderly and the physically disabled through LIXIL products and services, as well as harnessing the intelligence and perspectives of LIXIL's diverse workforce, as an engine for growth and innovation.

What emerged from the initial process of articulation was not so much a full purpose statement, but a clear direction that became the core framework for talking about our purpose. Through the assimilation and activation activities that followed, the goal would be to rally stakeholders, starting with employees, around these commitments and more closely integrate with the core business, thus moving purpose closer to the core strategy.

ASSIMILATE

At LIXIL, for the process of assimilation to be successful, it would be critical that the new CR framework and purpose were not regarded by employees from newly integrated companies as purely a LIXIL Japan initiative. If the intention was for purpose to be a key driver of engagement and PMI, then assimilation across group companies and regions and securing buy-in from all employees and stakeholders would be key.

To achieve this, we adopted a 360-degree approach to assimilation, seeking to embed the purpose mindset in all aspects of the company's value chain, from governance, to strategy, manufacturing, design, customer engagement and employee communications.

From a governance perspective, the CRC was established, which became an official part of the LIXIL Group's governance processes feeding into the Executive Officers Committee and Board. The CRC is made up of C-suite executives such as the CFO, CHRO, CTO, CLO and others. The committee meets every quarter, with the CR team within Public Affairs serving as the secretariat and the Chief Public Affairs Officer as the Chair. Among other things, the CRC reviews and approves sustainability targets and commitments, reviews progress against these commitments, considers proposals for LIXIL to extend its CR agenda, such as seeking participation in sustainability indices, as well as formulating new policies that support the company's CR commitments, such as a new diversity policy, etc. The CRC mechanism ensures that the commitments and strategy are officially assimilated into the institution through governance, and do not become victim to the whims of one department, one person or a small group of people.

Once formalized through the CRC, the process then began to be assimilated into the strategies across group businesses and regions. In many cases, these businesses had their own existing CR programs, so the framework and process of assimilation had to be flexible enough for all businesses to be able to take some ownership of, and for their initiatives to ladder up and contribute to, the bigger goals.

LIXIL's business is much broader than just sanitary ware and toilets. For example, in the case of the housing products business in Japan, producing window sashes or housing interiors, many within the business felt far removed from the sanitation and hygiene initiatives. However, the scope of the second pillar, Water Conservation and Environmental Sustainability and the third pillar, Diversity and Inclusion, was intentionally set in such a way that initiatives relevant to the housing business would be assimilated such as Universal Design or energy conservation through temperature control in the home.

In the case of the third CR pillar of Diversity and Inclusion, one example of assimilation was the company's focus on universal design (UD), an approach whereby products and services should support comfortable living for all people. To further promote these activities, LIXIL launched a special project team led by senior managers, bringing together a diverse selection of members from across the company to help formulate advanced UD concepts and a framework for future UD promotion.

With a clear CR strategy and firm commitments in place, further work was done to clarify and update LIXIL's purpose statement, resulting in, "making better homes a reality for everyone, everywhere".

The purpose statement provided clarity on the company's higher aim, and captured the full scope of the business, from the work done by brands such as GROHE in Europe or INAX in Japan, through to the SATO brand's affordable solutions for emerging economies.

Purpose messaging was firmly assimilated within corporate communications activities in Japan and globally, including an updated corporate narrative. Particularly outside of Japan, where LIXIL is the corporate brand and not used in the marketing of products, purpose became an important way to build awareness for what the LIXIL brand stood for, and a key point of differentiation from others within the industry. Thought leadership campaigns helped amplify LIXIL's activities and build the company's credibility as a leading voice on topics such as sanitation and hygiene, for example, with campaigns around World Toilet Day, where LIXIL worked with partners such as UNICEF to host events and media engagements, as well as LIXIL's involvement at TICAD VI (the Tokyo International Conference on African Development) in Nairobi, where the company launched a research report analyzing the true economic cost of poor sanitation.

Critically, the purpose agenda was also adopted into LIXIL's Medium-Term Strategic Plan or MTP. In Japan, publicly listed companies typically issue an MTP, which is sponsored by the CEO of the company. The MTP's objective is to set out management's strategy and financial goals for the next three-year period, with specific targets annually. In LIXIL's case, the MTP announced in November 2017 was to cover the period from April 1 (start of the Japanese financial year) of 2018, until the end of March 2021.

Demonstrating the intention to fully assimilate the new purpose agenda, the first of four strategic pillars outlined in the new MTP was "Establish a Purpose-Driven Entrepreneurial Company for Sustainable Growth". Key objectives outlined within this pillar of the MTP included:

- Become a company that we can be proud of, evoking respect and passion, for example, through LIXIL's SATO brand of products and the innovative business-focused approach it was taking to tackling the sanitation crisis.
- Focus on three "LIXIL Behaviors" — Do the Right Thing, Work with Respect, and Experiment and Learn — which will be recognized and adopted across the group globally, as a way to unite employees around a simple code of behavior and drive competitiveness. The Behaviors would reflect our purpose in the way that we should act as part of LIXIL.
- Consistently redefine the business domain, reflecting the entrepreneurial mindset and commitment to experiment and learn.

By engaging employees and shaping mindset, this first pillar of the MTP was intended to be the foundation upon which the other strategic pillars would be built. After all, if we could not build a company where employees were engaged and taking pride in their company and work, how would we be expected to achieve other key aspects of the MTP, such as developing attractive and differentiated products or driving strategic marketing?

As a further step to build pride and engagement among employees in support of LIXIL's purpose agenda, in 2017 we launched the first LIXIL Community Day campaign, whereby employees around the world would, for the first time, be able to take time out of their day during the campaign period to participate in activities that gave back to the community. The program was endorsed by the CEO and coordinated with HR teams at all key businesses and regions. Employees could choose their own activities within their teams, on the sole condition that the activities supported one of the three pillars of LIXIL's CR strategy.

Having involved some 3,500 employees in 15 countries in its inaugural year in 2017, by the third year in 2019 LIXIL Community Day recorded the involvement of more than 15,000 employees, with projects happening across 33 different countries, contributing to the communities in which we operate. Details of local projects were also shared widely among employees on the company's internal social platform, generating widespread awareness and engagement and, based on the many comments of encouragement, a sense of camaraderie between colleagues crossing borders and cultures.

ACTIVATE

Activating for LIXIL means doing, talking and accelerating these activities by working with others, or: Product Innovation and Social Enterprise, Advocacy and Thought Leadership and Driving Strategic Partnerships.

In the area of sanitation and hygiene, where the company has so far built the greatest momentum, the first stage was product innovation and building the social enterprise. This included the development of the SATO range of high quality and affordable toilets targeted specifically at the base of the pyramid (BoP), as well as developing an R&D pipeline of other affordable off-grid toilet systems to serve the BOP. In addition, LIXIL adopted an innovative social enterprise business model to scale up the delivery of these products globally, rather than relying on philanthropy and CSR.

It was this "doing" that also gave LIXIL the credibility to expand its advocacy and thought leadership activities globally, with the aim of further raising awareness for the issue and positioning LIXIL as an authority in the industry. These advocacy and thought leadership activities included the development of a research report on the true economic cost of poor sanitation, which was launched to coincide with the Tokyo International Conference on African Development and World Water Week in 2016, and gave LIXIL a platform to discuss the sanitation issue beyond its product portfolio. LIXIL also hosted and participated in conferences with partners such as UNICEF, the World Toilet Organization, the Toilet Board Organization, WaterAid and others to highlight the issue of sanitation, and ran integrated thought leadership and profile-raising campaigns around World Toilet Day. It also made sanitation and hygiene its signature issue at the World Economic Forum, working with WEF to facilitate multilateral sessions on the topic at its Annual Meeting in Davos.

Finally, strategic partnerships are critical to accelerating the impact of LIXIL's activities. For instance, in 2018 LIXIL launched a unique new "shared value" partnership with UNICEF, under which the partners will leverage their relevant skills to tackle the sanitation challenge from both the demand (in UNICEF's case) and supply side (where LIXIL's products come in). Whereas Sustainable Development Goal 6, which aims to secure improved access to clean water and sanitation for all, has been lagging behind its goals, such partnerships seek to establish sustainable sanitation markets in developing countries and accelerate change.

Diagrammatically, these three areas are circular, because they feed into one another. For instance, the UNICEF partnership also build employee engagement and pride, and differentiates LIXIL with business partners and customers as a company that is serious about its purpose ambitions. We also designed a fundraising mechanism to support the UNICEF partnership which activates loyalty and support from employees, business partners and consumers. So, not only is the partnership itself working on helping us connect toilets with people who don't have them, but the way in which we are funding the partnership also helps the business and the company strengthen its relationship with these key stakeholders.

3 KEYS TO ACCELERATE GLOBAL SANITATION AND HYGIENE INITIATIVES

Providing toilets for two billion people who don't have access to safe and clean toilets

- High quality and affordable toilets, SATO
- R&D pipeline to develop other affordable off-grid toilet systems for BOP

Product innovation

Advocacy

Strategic Partnerships

- Advocacy for municipalities, governments and the civil society

- Strategic partnerships with UN organizations, foundations and NGOs

Develop sustainable sanitation market for developing countries

CONCLUSION

There is still much work to do to truly embed purpose across the organization and establish "one LIXIL" across the global organization of 70,000 employees. But when looking back on those key questions that were asked, such as "how do we build a sense of shared pride in LIXIL"?, "what does LIXIL stand for"? and "what is the shared vision beyond simply profits"?, the purpose agenda that was articulated, assimilated and activated within the company has gone a long way to providing answers to these questions, and building a unique identity for the company.

6. Mahindra Group (Mahindra): *Rise*

INTRODUCTION

Mahindra Group is a multinational conglomerate, headquartered in Mumbai, Maharashtra, India. Founded in 1945, its operations commenced with steel trading. The group has grown significantly from its initial business to many diverse business verticals, expanding its operations in over 100 countries around the globe. By 1994, the Group had become so diverse that it undertook a fundamental reorganization, dividing its businesses into six Strategic Business Units: Automotive; Farm Equipment; Infrastructure; Trade and Financial Services; Information Technology and Automotive Components. Currently, Mahindra & Mahindra is one of the 20 largest companies in India and spans 22 different industries.

Over the past eight decades, the Group has created substantial value for shareholders through a judicious combination of expansion, productivity improvement and strategic partnerships, resulting in considerable growth. The Group has a legacy of moving in tandem with societies' needs, they have stepped in and helped to create a new line of business in new sectors just as an emerging economy required it. When India required robust vehicles for rural transportation, Mahindra started in the UV space. As India's agrarian sector necessitated mechanization and a reduced dependence on foreign imports, Mahindra forayed into farm equipment; a move that was quickly followed by the wave later known as India's agriculture revolution. They were also the first movers in

Information Technology, becoming torchbearers of the IT revolution in India. The Group now focuses on developing alternate energy sources because it believes energy conservation will play a huge role in ensuring a better future – not just for India and the communities in India, but for the entire world. Over the years the individual companies in the Mahindra Group had their own mission statements and cultures. As the group expanded globally, these statements showed limitations in being relevant in the global arena and across the businesses that had been developed since the company was formed. There was a need to connect with global stakeholders by staying relevant locally across the world while maintaining a culturally diverse workforce.

In January 2011, the Mahindra Group launched a new corporate brand and purpose under the banner of "Mahindra Rise" to unify Mahindra's image across industries and geographies. It stems from Mahindra's legacy of creating shared value within the lives of their stakeholders and building the industries that are the foundations of a nation's economic growth. Their new core purpose was articulated as: **"We will challenge conventional thinking and innovatively use our resources to drive positive change in the lives of our stakeholders and communities across the world to enable them to Rise"**. The primary objective of its core purpose is to drive positive change in the lives of its stakeholders and communities by enabling them to rise by challenging conventional thinking and by innovatively using their resources. In every business vertical within the Mahindra Group, this one sentence is the mother fount and driver of all their business and human capital strategies.

ARTICULATE

Mahindra had a purpose statement prior to 2011 which had lasted for a couple of decades. It read, "Indians are second to none in the world". The growth and progress of Mahindra very closely mirrored the growth and progress of India as a young country. India achieved independence from the British in 1947 and Mahindra was set up in 1945. In the wake of a newly born national identity, the initial purpose statement was inspired by the founders of the company passionately believing in India and wanting to prove to the world that Mahindra had the ability to produce quality products and render services that were second to none. However by 1990, Mahindra had considerable presence beyond India. Mr. Ruzbeh Irani, President, Group Human Resources for the Mahindra Group shared:

> "It was all very well as long as Mahindra was essentially an Indian company. As we went into global expansion, having a purpose statement which talked about Indians being second-to-none in the world no longer made sense for a global company. We had diverse nationalities employed in our various offices. With a global footprint of the Mahindra brand, for our non-Indian employees to say that their purpose was to prove that Indians are second to none really did not resonate. Hence, we embarked on an exercise to redefine our purpose in 2009".

To support its initiative and redefine its purpose, the group sought assistance from a boutique advertising agency called Strawberry Frog, based in the United States. The owner of this agency, Scott Goodson, had met the then Vice Chairman and Managing Director, Mr. Anand Mahindra, and visited the headquarters in Mumbai. Goodson shared with Mr. Mahindra that he felt there was something unique about the group. He advised the Chairman that he should take a serious look at how the brand positioned itself globally. He added that there was a compelling reason why the people in the organization came to work. This should be explored and brought to the forefront of Mahindra with a unifying brand idea. Mr. Mahindra and the leadership team found great merit in redefining both their brand and their purpose to resonate with one another. The leadership team was anyway already debating and discussing as to what their purpose was at that point in time. What followed was the launch of a study in 3 phases:

1. An internal interview process with managers and focus group discussions across the group to unearth people's goals and values as well as their perceptions of the company.
2. Studies to understand how the outside world perceived India and Indians.
3. A societal trend study that included ethnographic interviews and discussion groups with customers in key markets.

The key leaders at the Mahindra Group revisited the core purpose in a bid to unify all their businesses. During the iterative design process, the strategy team met regularly with Mr. Anand Mahindra. From the conversations, it became clear that "purpose" had the potential not only to re-position the Mahindra brand but also to catalyze an internal cultural transformation. Mr. Irani recalled one of the challenges they encountered as they were researching their core purpose:

"Our research commenced immediately after the financial crisis of 2008. In 2009–10, when we were in the thick of our research, one aspect became loud and clear… That was the lack of trust and a huge trust deficit. The average person on the road did not trust governments or large corporates. We recognized the importance of a company with a purpose that people could genuinely trust was even more crucial than earlier, or under normal circumstances. Now 10 years wiser, we also recognize that by virtue of having a value-centred core purpose and talking about it and living it, you attract the kind of people who buy into that purpose. Today, a lot of millennials want to work for a company with a purpose. A lot of consumers want to buy only from a company with a purpose, and not just any purpose, but a purpose that matches their own values. The people we hired during that phase, their actions, both internal and external, the businesses we progressively got into, are all examples of us living RISE through business, and to me that is the most powerful way to live your core purpose. You attract the right people then, and it becomes self-perpetuating".

As they embarked on articulating the purpose to their employees, the leadership team was aware that it was paramount to get their people to buy into the brand ideology. They had to encourage their employees to have a mind-set to seize opportunities and fight challenges to create competitive advantages. It was also the prerogative of the leadership team to create a climate that promoted innovation. To make that happen, the HR team began documenting innovations across the group. Mr. Irani was also able to share with the senior leaders how their study indicated that customers across the world had expressed a common optimism about the future and shared a common desire to "Rise" — to succeed and create a better future for themselves.

ASSIMILATE

"Rise" and its tenets were already embedded into the Mahindra culture. Mahindra did not encounter any resistance to the assimilation of the new purpose. According to Irani, Rise was "who they were, who they are and who they aspire to be". Mr. Anand Mahindra had put it very succinctly during the launch of Rise when he said: "What we are doing is converting a subtext into a headline". These powerful words amplified the need for the purpose to be assimilated across every business vertical and region where Mahindra had a presence. Mr. Irani added that if it was a concept that they had brought in from the outside, the purpose would have been a lot more difficult to take root across the group.

Mahindra, Goodson and Irani began by getting the entire leadership team of the Mahindra Group — which had all the presidents and members of the Group Executive Board – to come together. Irani was serving as the Chief Brand Officer of the Group during the period of the three-phased study. The leaders from across the Group embarked on an aggressive communication campaign to spread the launch of Rise. The core team first conducted a large-scale interactive process with the top 300 leaders of the Mahindra Group. Coined as "Living the Brand", the workshops socialized the new core purpose and the stories associated with it. This was then cascaded across the different business verticals.

As Irani recalled the assimilation of Rise across verticals, he said:

"We decided to break down the elements of Rise rather than just stating the Core Purpose. We talked about the three tenets of "Rise" which were (i) Accepting No Limits, (ii) Alternative Thinking and (iii) Driving Positive Change. This was what brought it to life and got the buy in from the businesses. We created the House of Rise from these tenets. The foundation of the House were the 5 core values of the Mahindra Group. These 5 core values have been with us ever since we were established — they are immutable. At the Group Executive Board, I remember debating if we should alter these core values in any way. We came to a decision that the core values are core — we were born with these values; these define us and there's no question of changing them. They are in fact, the foundation of the House of Rise. If we do anything, the ultimate filter through which we need to pass is our 5 core values, which are: dignity of the individual, professionalism, customer-first, quality focused and good corporate citizenship. Very basic, very fundamental".

The leadership team spent considerable hours aligning all the HR levers with these three pillars. Since people experience behaviors, the leadership team decided it was important to articulate the behaviors — aligned with the three pillars and the 5 core values. This could be demonstrated and emulated by the larger group of

Mahindra employees. They were clear that it had to start from the top — the leadership team had to demonstrate the behaviors and effortlessly bring the pillars to life. The three pillars and the five behaviors became the 3 + 5 framework that guides everything at Mahindra, especially all leadership and human capital initiatives. The five behaviors are: (i) Ability to use the whole mind: In any situation, to combine the left brain of logic, intellect and rationality, with the right brain of empathy, connection, intuition and innovation. (ii) Being a multiplier: To do more with less where people's energies are multiplied, and there is greater passion and engagement to create a sense of ownership. (iii) Managing fear and leveraging failure: Helping to overcome fear by understanding that taking risks and experimentation all lead to learnings from the failure. (iv) Mindfulness: Being open to all the possibilities that exist in any situation and not being a prisoner of the past, either of success or failure. (v) Trust: The ability to create trust by speaking the truth and walking the talk.

Mahindra's House of Rise

The *House of Rise* helped the process of communication. Rise and its tenets were embedded in the decision-making of all the business and HR leaders. These metrics were considered during recruitment, induction, on boarding, performance management, promotions and the assessment of other leadership competencies. The most important aspect was to "walk the talk". Senior leaders were given the responsibility to reflect the *Rise* values and strengthen the culture. Doing that consciously, both communicating it and living it on a day-to-day basis made the words come to life. The annual awards were rebranded as "Rise" awards, with the categories celebrating the tenets of Rise.

At Mahindra, the decision-making process is aligned with the tenets of Rise. For example, any Mahindra business that embarks into a

new business venture is guided by the Rise philosophy. Rise was behind Mahindra's decision to enter the renewable energy business. A decision like this has the objective of driving positive change in communities while generating profits for the company. Rise inspires in employees a sense of meaning, by framing their work in terms of the impact it makes on society. Rise, as a purpose, has offered a sense of meaning and a passion for the Mahindra employees. Employees have become creative to design and deliver services that are good for business and society. This has led to sustainable performance and attracting people to be the champions of driving positive change. There exists a virtuous cycle of growth and Mahindra feels this is a recipe that can be adopted by any corporation to create win–win outcomes. The business decisions made by the different verticals within the conglomerate stand as a testimony to the fact that the three pillars are not just words on the wall — they are actually embedded within the DNA of Mahindra employees.

ACTIVATE

There are many pockets of excellence within Mahindra that reflect the activation of Rise. Many stories emerge from the Mahindra offices across the country and these stories stand out as powerful testimonies to the activation of Rise. *Rise* helped to differentiate Mahindra from other businesses by emphasizing its role as an outstanding corporate citizen. Mr. Irani added,

> "The fact of the matter is — if we look at the businesses we are in, and the way we have gone about doing these businesses — these tenets are reflected. We are the largest rural-focused non-banking financial company in India, and we started with a unique model where we went out and gave loans to the unbankable. These are the people without credit history and who would have to go to money lenders to be able to buy an asset. Our financial services company found a way to reliably give them loans. Initially, the loans were issued against the purchase of our tractors, or our commercial vehicles. We gave them the ability to earn an income and use that income to repay the loan, and then become an owner of an asset that would give them income for the rest of their lives. In doing so, we used the 3 pillars — of accepting no limits by challenging the status quo — "extending loans to the unbankable". Alternative thinking was established by using a new business model by our financial services business where they used the services of employees who are entrenched in the community. These were our people who knew the community well enough and could gauge who were those who were likely to return the money and who were not. They overcame the challenge of dealing with rural India where there was no formal credit-rating score. It exists now but not during the time we commenced our business. The third pillar, driving positive change lies in the

fact that we enabled these customers of ours to earn an income and be able to stand on their own feet as a result of the loans".

Mahindra Finance helps farmers buy Mahindra tractors and pickup trucks and even build homes. Mahindra Lifespaces has been working to develop eco-friendly real estate. Instead of applying only cement to surface-coat building roofs, it uses an additional layer of broken ceramic tiles over the cement, which helps to bounce off light and minimize heat absorption. Another example is when India experienced a fuel crisis in the 1970s. That is when the automobile business unit converted their diesel engines into gensets to combat the power shortage in India. This led to the creation of a new business line within Mahindra called Mahindra Powerol.

The multitude of examples within the Mahindra Group stand as testimony that Rise has resulted in innovations and creativity from Mahindra employees that benefit a larger group of stakeholders. By bringing its corporate social responsibility, sustainability and corporate governance initiatives under the branding umbrella "Rise for Good", Mahindra has added impetus, momentum and synergy to the activation of Rise by its employees.

Mahindra prides itself on strategic CSR initiatives with three signature programs: (1) Nanhi Kali — one of India's largest programs that enables underprivileged girls to complete 10 years of schooling. The project provides daily academic support as well as an annual school supplies kit, which allow the girls to attend school with dignity. (2) Mahindra Pride Schools — which recruit semi-educated youth from the slums and train them to secure corporate jobs, thereby ensuring livelihood training for socially and economically marginalized youth and (3) Hariyali — which plants a million trees every year to increase the green cover and provide lifelong supply of clean oxygen to millions of people. Every tree helps to combat climate change, and the Hariyali tribe continues to grow year after year.

With India on the brink of the third stage of COVID transmission, the Chairman, Mr. Mahindra, offered his entire salary for the year to help with the setting up of facilities to deal with the crisis. With the alarming number of people infected with COVID-19 in India, the nation would face a huge shortage of medical infrastructure. To help in that hour of need, Mahindra put his company's manufacturing facilities to work on producing ventilators. Mahindra also offered the resorts of Mahindra Holidays to be used as temporary healthcare facilities. In addition, the Mahindra Group's project team stands ready to help the Indian Army or the Government to set up temporary care facilities. At the time of writing this chapter, the group was discussing the creation of a fund via the Mahindra Foundation. The fund would lend financial support to small businesses and the self-employed population that have borne the maximum brunt of the crisis.

The Government of India considers the Mahindra Group as an outstanding corporate citizen. For his contribution to the field of trade and industry, in 2020 Mr. Anand Mahindra was awarded the "Padma Bhushan", the third-highest civilian award conferred by the Govt of India, by Prime Minister Narendra Modi. While accepting the award, Mr. Mahindra tweeted this response:

> "Trying to do well AND do good. And there's an old saying: If you see a turtle on top of a fence, you know for sure it didn't get there on its own! I stand on the shoulders of all Mahindraites. I will convey your compliments to them"!

CONCLUSION

It has been a decade since Mahindra articulated their revised purpose. The company has achieved considerable success and international recognition for having lived up to its purpose. However, the mood within Mahindra is one where the company leaders do not believe they have reached the zenith of achieving their redefined purpose. A Harvard Business Review article on "Put Purpose as the Core of your Strategy" summed up how the group has effectively managed to redefine their purpose by using a retrospective and prospective approach. Mahindra used a retrospective approach by reflecting on the past and using an internal discovery process. They also used the prospective approach, where the Mahindra leaders looked ahead to take stock of the broader ecosystem and assessed their potential for impact in it. With a clear vision for the future and a compelling reason for being, Mahindra geared their organization with a revised and refined purpose of Rise. As ardent followers of the concept of "shared value" and "collaboration", Mahindra has shown to the world that meeting the unmet needs of underserved customers in underpenetrated markets can drive business as well as positive change.

7. Olam International (Olam): *Re-imagining Global Agriculture and Food Systems*

INTRODUCTION

Olam International, otherwise known as a "corporate farmer", is a leading food and agri-business, supplying food ingredients, feed and fiber to thousands of customers worldwide, ranging from multi-national organizations with world famous brands to small family run businesses. Established in 1989, Olam is listed on the Singapore Exchange and comprises 87,600 full-time, seasonal and contract employees spanning its businesses such as Cocoa, Coffee, Cotton, Edible Nuts and Spices across the world. While growing its own crops in its own orchards and estates, and sourcing from around 5 million farmers globally, it also operates over 180 processing facilities and 14 innovation centers.

As an entity, Olam plays multiple roles — as a farmer, processor, supplier, expert and as a "re-imagineer". Olam's purpose has stemmed from the re-imagining exercise undertaken by its employees. As an agriculture-based industry, the sector faces huge environmental and social challenges. Olam's plantation and processing experiences, coupled with its year-round presence working with farmers in remote regions, elevates it to a position to re-imagine global agriculture for the better. It has a vision to create living landscapes where prosperous farmers and thriving communities live in harmony creating healthy ecosystems. With a clearly defined purpose as **"Re-imagining Global Agriculture and Food Systems"**, Olam aims to address the many challenges involved in meeting the needs of a growing global population, while achieving positive impact for farming communities, the planet and all its stakeholders.

Olam has identified four key trends and opportunities underpinning the food and agri-sector which have influenced its strategies for growth. Driven by consumers and advances in technology, these trends include increasing demand for healthier foods, traceable and sustainable sourcing, ecommerce and the rise of "purpose" brands. The trends that were pinned down to help Olam make informed decisions were: (i) Right for me, (ii) Right for the planet, Right for the Producer, (iii) How I live and Consume and (iv) How it is produced. Based on these four trends, Olam has developed four strategic pathways for growth aligned with their purpose of "Re-imagine Global Agriculture and Food Systems".

ARTICULATE

Being a three decade old company, Olam has always focused on fulfilling the needs and wants of its stakeholders. Mr. Anantharaman Shekhar, Executive Director and CEO, Olam Food Ingredients, shared with us, "During our various discussions, it was clear that our stakeholders increasingly expect our entities to be purpose-led, a force for good, an agent of change, a company that puts social and environmental issues at the center of the strategy, and not as a separate sustainability or CSR initiative. While creating a purpose and living by this purpose is not entirely new to Olam, our association with the agriculture sector meant taking responsibility for some of the world's biggest economic and environmental challenges. It is a tragic truth that millions of farmers, particularly smallholders, who grow cash crops like cocoa, cashew and coffee, live at or below subsistence levels, while natural resources, such as soil and forests, are being degraded or lost at an alarming rate. Compounding it is the fact that around a third of all food produced is lost or wasted".

With the world population set to increase by 2 billion by 2050, Shekhar and his team were cognizant that they could not carry on business as usual. Tackling the issues impacting the environment was a herculean task. While Olam had many sustainability programs in place, it was evident that it had to go beyond what was happening in the present. The company decided on collective action plans as an organization to step on the accelerator so as to secure the future of its businesses and protect its stakeholders.

Shekhar believes that Olam has been a "Values-driven, Purpose-led" organization since its inception. Olam, being an agri-based company, had its origins of growing its business from emerging markets with a predominant presence in rural communities. Right from inception, Shekhar reiterated how values and purpose have stayed at the core of their business model to make Olam a sustainable organization. During the years 2012–2017, Olam was guided by a purpose statement which was articulated as "Growing Responsibly" — a mantra that ran throughout all its commercial, social and environmental initiatives. It was reflected in its Board meetings, governance processes, the award-winning Olam Livelihood Charter and embedded in the various programs undertaken by Olam where it explained its activities on generating prosperity, contributing to social wellbeing and looking after the natural resources wherever it operated.

The articulation of Olam's current purpose statement — "Re-imagining Global Agriculture & Food Systems" — came about in 2017. The company recognized that the earlier purpose statement on "Growing Responsibly" was more about how it did its businesses. Olam executives concluded that there had to be a more inspiring, motivating and compelling reason for people to come to work every day, across all their global operations. After extensive internal and external consultations with all its key stake-holders, and given the huge sector challenges outlined above, Olam redefined its purpose as "Re-imagining Global Agriculture and Food Systems" to be in tune with the times and with a focus on delivering three outcomes: (i) Prosperous Farmers & Food Systems: Re-designing farming and food value chains so that all participants get adequately compensated and profit fairly from their respective investments and efforts within the value chain, (ii) Thriving communities: Revitalizing communities who depend on agricultural and food systems so that entire communities can raise their overall standard of living and wellness (including health, hygiene, education, etc.) and (iii) Re-generation of the Living World: Regenerating nature and restoring the balance between agriculture and environmental ecosystems and living landscapes.

Olam has successfully articulated this purpose as the key link to achieve its strategic priorities and sustainability initiatives. With issues like climate change and water scarcity are being discussed at international forums, Olam understands that these are significant trends that will impact Olam in the long run. The right climate and adequate water are critical for cultivation and any imbalance will impact the yield of the produce. Olam therefore holds itself responsible for the plight of the farmers across the world to achieve a viable livelihood. In doing so, Olam ensures that the actions taken now are aligned to producing food and ingredients that are Right for the Planet, Right for the Producer and Right for Consumer. Olam has identified four enablers to achieve its vision of being the most differentiated and valuable food and agri-business by 2040, aligned with its purpose. Accordingly, Olam has refreshed its strategy to achieve its 2040 vision on changing the consumer landscape by continuing to: (a) Invest in its capabilities to enhance its leadership position, (b) Invest and capitalize on the key emerging trends of health and wellness, traceability and sustainability, (c) Focusing on furthering its leadership in its chosen businesses and creating greater value for its shareholders, customers, suppliers, employees and partners.

Shekhar elaborated, "What this means is an organization-wide focus on how we, as a company, can help produce more food, feed and fibre with significantly fewer resources, reduced food waste, enhanced biodiversity, tackling climate change and transforming farmer livelihoods. We have converted this into an overall organizational framework, which starts with our core purpose and the three outcomes; identified 10 material areas where we have the relevant expertise to make meaningful impact; linked each of these material areas with specific Sustainable Development Goals as prescribed by the United Nations and identified the various policies, standards, programs and partnerships that underpin our focus and actions across all our operations globally".

This framework compiled by Olam is depicted as follows:

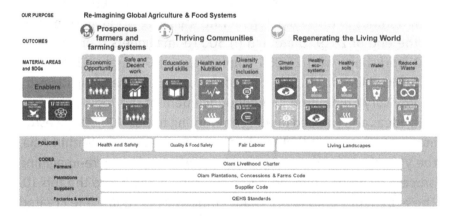

ASSIMILATE

Olam's current purpose statement, though relatively new, secured the complete buy-in from the leadership team at the top. Today, this purpose statement is driven through every level of leadership and cascades to every profit center across various businesses and geographies. Having been associated with Olam for more than two decades, it is clear to Shekhar that having a purpose and working towards achieving and living the purpose is integral to the future of Olam's agri supply chains, which consist of sourcing raw materials and transforming them to deliver food, feed and fibre to the world. This value chain gets complicated with the rapidly changing consumer preferences for food and ingredients with customers exerting greater emphasis on health & nutritional value. This makes Olam play a pivotal role in clean labeling, authenticity, supply chain visibility and sustainability to meet the rapidly evolving preferences of the consumers.

Throughout 2018 and 2019, some of the brightest minds across Olam embarked on a program to live their purpose and brainstorm solutions to the systemic issues faced by the agriculture sector. Together, a group of 500 Re-imagineers (Olam employees) from across the business helped to generate an array of innovative ideas with the power to transform food systems, help farmers to prosper, communities to thrive and regenerate the living world. In summary, by the end of 2019, Olam had (i) 500 re-imagineers trained to run 660 workshops with 24,000 employees, (ii) Generated 1,200 "re-imagining" ideas, (iii) Selection of the top 25 re-imagining ideas by an Advisory Committee, (iv) Announcement of the Top 10 re-imagining ideas and (v) Seed funding amounting to US$ 400,000 invested in these 10 projects that made a good business case. Within Asia, the Vietnam team demonstrated huge passion for the re-imagining process by getting two ideas into the top 25 and 1 into the top 10. The experience among the Olam employees to re-imagine created an environment of openness and a sense of belonging, breaking hierarchies and generating innovative ideas related to current processes that could be enhanced. In doing so, Olam has really demonstrated how a purpose led organization can have an infectious growth pattern where every aspect of the business and all employees are aligned with the purpose.

In explaining how every Olam employee has assimilated the purpose, Shekhar elaborated, "Purpose can only be achieved and ring true with stakeholders (both employees and external stakeholders) when it is integral to the overall business strategy and is embedded in such a way that it becomes part of our day-to-day operations and ways of working. A good example is our product AtSource — which helps commercialize and scale our sustainability capabilities. We believe AtSource to be the most comprehensive sustainable sourcing solution for B2B customers. From field to factory gate, AtSource helps customers shape change on the ground and meet multiple social and environmental targets, increasing resilience in supply chains. By connecting customers directly to the source of supply at each stage of the product's journey, traceability is guaranteed. Our offer builds across 3 tiers with progressively enhanced levels of impact, verification, insight and information, culminating in transformational change. A digital dashboard provides instant access to rich data, advanced foot-printing and granular traceability. Highly targeted interventions can then improve economic, social and environmental factors. Developing AtSource from a minimum viable product to a now successful product across more than 100 customers is a great example of how Olam is living its Purpose".

With a strong focus on purpose-led behaviors across Olam, Shekhar shared how it was important to ensure that purpose is not just the remit of the corporate sustainability team. Every department in

Olam, from Finance to Logistics to Trading, plays a part. The Treasury team secures sustainability KPI-linked loans; the Finance team takes the lead on accounting for sustainability through the development of the Olam Integrated Impact Statement; and the Digital Olam function has made huge headway in identifying disruptive business opportunities like the AtSource described earlier.

ACTIVATE

Olam was able to activate its redefined purpose "Re-imagine Global Agriculture and Food Systems" across its value chain with both internal and external stakeholders since it had invested considerable time and resources supporting smallholders and driving environmental improvements across the region, particularly around mitigating and adapting to climate change. Now and then there are some tensions and discords that occur between leaders within Olam as to whether the investment in the company's purpose is apt, exceeds expectations or is below expectation. As a business, the senior leaders are also responsible for ensuring commercial viability within their verticals. As a food and agri-business, Olam realizes that it can't solve all of the developmental challenges, like health, poverty and education issues, alone in the regions where it operates. All these challenges Olam faces go beyond the agri sector and therefore require the involvement of multiple partners from governments to banks to NGOs in the various countries it operates in. This is where a clearly articulated and highly assimilated purpose helps to attract external stakeholders and join hands to deliver on projects for the larger good, thus helping Olam to activate its purpose.

Olam understands that partnerships with external organizations are the key to growing their footprint. Partnerships bring in scale and expertise. Some examples where partnerships have helped Olam to meet the shared purpose of all stakeholders impacting the commercial, social and environmental goals in Asia are the collaboration with: (i) International Finance Corporation (IFC), Hindustan Lever and Solidaridad to develop sugarcane fields in India, (ii) Nespresso to cultivate high quality Arabica in Indonesia and (iii) IFC and Japan International Cooperation Agency (JICA) to build a facility in Vietnam and Indonesia to provide support, stability and reliable market access to smallholder farmers. All these collaborations have helped Olam to activate their core purpose of re-imagining global agriculture and food systems by fulfilling the mandate of enabling inclusive economic growth with environmental stewardship and regional integration.

Another powerful example emerging from Olam on activating its purpose is around the Sustainable Rice Platform work (SRP), a multi-stakeholder platform established in December 2011. The SRP is co-convened by UN Environment and the International Rice Research Institute (IRRI) to promote resource efficiency and sustainability in trade flows production and consumption operations, and supply chains in the global rice sector. The SRP pursues public policy development and voluntary market transformation initiatives to provide private, non-profit and public actors in the global rice sector with sustainable production standards and outreach mechanisms that contribute to increasing the global supply of affordable rice, improved livelihoods for rice producers and reduced environmental impact of rice production. Olam has served as a founding member of SRP. The efforts of the team from Olam's headquarters in Singapore have helped SRP be among the short-listed organizations for a US$100 million grant from the MacArthur Foundation for improving the livelihoods of 500,000 rice farmers while reducing environmental impacts.

A couple of other examples include opening up Olam's technology to Wildlife Conservation Society (WCS) to protect Bukit Barisan Selatan National Park in Indonesia from deforestation by farmers, and training 900 Christian pastors in COVID sanitization to reach coffee farmers across Papua New Guinea where faith and farming are the two important aspects of local life. These activities stand testimony to how re-imagining global agriculture and food systems depends on big partnerships and driving change across the agri sector.

Olam is also clear that "Re-imagining" must lead to business benefit — there must be a commercial value to Olam, while bringing value to other stakeholders. One such innovation that deserves mention is the tool "Olam Direct", which was first piloted in Indonesia. Olam Direct connects participants in the supply chain and enables the end-to-end flow of information and produce. Each app interfaces directly with users and is designed for their needs. Olam aims to create an industry leading platform that helps connect millions of farmers directly with Olam to ensure a fair and transparent sourcing process. This was done with Olam investing several hours with smallholder farmers to identify their main pain points related to improved market access and transparent pricing and negotiation. Today, farmers irrespective of phone type or internet connectivity can transact through the Olam Direct platform. By embarking on this initiative, Olam aims to create an ecosystem for transaction while also delivering sustainability, agronomy advisory, and weather and inputs information. Piloted in Indonesia, Olam Direct will be cascaded to other parts of the world.

Olam's 2019 Annual Report details additional exciting initiatives that demonstrate it activating its purpose. Olam has launched a range of consumer purpose brands putting sustainability at the heart of its business. These actions taken by Olam help the company behave like a catalyst towards making sustainable consumption behavior the new normal. Olam has the rich experience and subject matter expertise to explore the sweet spot of (a) what consumers want, (b) what the planet needs and (c) what Olam is good at. The focus over 2019 was understanding consumer attitudes and actions around packaged food, the environment and supporting local communities. Having identified potential opportunities, Olam is now fleshing out the unique brand proposition and developing and testing launch products. Of course, no company can launch a purpose brand unless people believe that the company is indeed "living its purpose", which Olam is aiming for.

With Olam's 30th year anniversary under its belt, and the dawn of a new chapter for Olam, Olam too expected a buoyant 2020. With the world battling the pandemic, Olam realized that these are testing times without a clear indication on the consequences the pandemic will have on its supply chains in particular and the business in general. Olam had a two-pronged approach — short term and long term. While in the short-term they continue to work with customers, governments and communities on COVID-19 contingency planning to protect public health and minimize impacts of the demand shock and disruptions to supply, they are also adapting to the strong possibility that normality as commonly known might not return for some time to come. Hence, as part of their long-term objectives, they have begun to identify new ways of living, working and conducting business while at the same time looking for opportunities to unlock value for Olam and all its stakeholders. The foundations that Olam has built over the last 30 years will hopefully pivot Olam's role to the centre of delivering food, feed and fibre to the world. Never before has a purpose to "Re-imagine Global Agriculture and Food Systems" been so critical.

CONCLUSION

Every day the farming and food system feeds and clothes 7.5 billion people. This is a testament to the efforts and ingenuity of farmers and other participants across the food and agri ecosystem. Olam is aware that the current production and consumption of food is not sustainable. Hence, they have redefined their purpose to re-imagine a better system that properly meets the nutritional needs of a future population of an estimated 10 billion people (2050). Olam aims to be a player in this ecosystem to deliver sufficient income for farmers and their families and produce all the food and fibre they need within the limits and constraints posed by the natural environment. Across Olam offices all over the world, Olam employees understand the importance of reputation — the efforts and time taken to build one and how easily it can be tarnished or eroded. Therefore, engagement with various external stakeholders to build understanding and develop trust has remained critical.

With the numerous re-imagined ideas that are being implemented, Olam believes that the sector can rise up and deliver all of this and more. Olams's purpose will go a long way to achieving three outcomes. First, to have thriving communities consisting of a class of prosperous farmers and food systems. Secondly, to rethink how people and companies are financially rewarded to make the agricultural sector attractive and viable. Finally, the regeneration of the living world by re-generating ecosystems, soils and water to create landscapes where industrial agriculture, smallholders and other rural commerce co-exist with nature.

8. Prudential Assurance Co (Prudential): *Innovating to Help Everyone Live Well*

INTRODUCTION

Prudential was founded as "The Prudential Investment, Loan and Assurance Association" in 1848 in London, United Kingdom. In Singapore, Prudential started out as an agent for fire insurance in 1924 before it attained full branch status and began operations as the Prudential Assurance Company Singapore ("Prudential Singapore") from 1931, a century after Singapore became the capital of the British Straits Settlements. Prudential Singapore functions as an indirect wholly-owned subsidiary of UK-based, Prudential plc, and is one of the top life insurance companies in the country. The company provides well-rounded financial solutions to customers through their multi-channel distribution network, with product offerings in protection, savings and investment. Prudential also has an AA- rating from leading credit agency, Standard & Poor.

From 2016 onwards, the Singapore office began a series of activities in a bid to transform itself. Prior to 2016, the office was traditional — characterized by closed doors, offices for the leadership team and desks separated by partitions. The then CEO of Prudential Singapore, Mr. Wilfred Blackburn, decided to make sweeping changes to the company's culture to one that is fit for the future. In embarking on the transformation, Mr. Blackburn actively sought the support of everyone in the organization, as he believed the culture of the company must be owned by its employees. Over many hours of brainstorming and discussions where every employee was given a chance to express themselves, the purpose statement of Prudential Singapore was born: Innovating to help everyone live well. This purpose is supported by a clear set of values which was also co-created by the employees and define the ways of working among colleagues.

Today, a walk around the revamped office space is a treat to one's eyes. The traditional symbols of hierarchy — cubicles and assigned seating — have disappeared. The CEO does not have an office but a locker like every other employee. Gone are the days where the leadership team is "hidden" behind doors. Today, senior leaders are more accessible to their colleagues. The revamped office design was part of the plan to create a more collaborative and empowered workplace that supports the corporate values and celebrates its culture.

ARTICULATE

Prudential Singapore's efforts towards articulating a purpose statement commenced in 2017 under the leadership of the then CEO, Mr. Wilfred Blackburn, by which time Prudential Singapore already had an established 85-year legacy in the country. As a brand, Prudential Singapore is well entrenched in life insurance, but the organization had reached a stage of maturity where leaders started asking themselves questions about not "who we have been" but "who we were going to be". Ms. Sheela Parakkal, CHRO of Prudential Singapore, reminisced those days as she shared with us,

> "We had reached a stage where we could no longer look back on our achievements but needed to look further ahead into the future. It was this forward-thinking approach that got us to review our relevance in the market and to re-define our culture.

We wanted to make sure we have another century of leadership going forward. And so, our work around purpose began".

While Prudential Singapore was successful in its 85-year history in Singapore, the life insurer was challenged on several fronts — rapid digitalization of the economy and rising customer expectations. In order for Prudential Singapore to emerge stronger and more successful amid the challenges, the leadership team knew it needed a strong purpose to unite and to rally its people. And this purpose had to be co-created for it to be embraced and celebrated. Hence, everyone who was in the company then had a say in developing and articulating the purpose statement of "innovating to help everyone live well".

Further analysis of Prudential Singapore's purpose statement can be broken down into three components. The first being around "innovating". This talks about how Prudential wants to function as a company — bold and pushing frontiers. This innovative spirit is especially important given the increased disruptions faced by the insurance industry. "To help everyone" conveys the human and caring side of what Prudential Singapore aims to be. It also represents how the company wants to be inclusive for everyone. "Live well" is the desired outcome. Prudential Singapore looks at wellness holistically. It is not just about health and finances, but overall well-being, including social, emotional, intellectual and environmental wellness.

In articulating the purpose, every employee at Prudential Singapore was asked to re-evaluate their work and look at it from the lens of "innovating to help everyone live well". The leadership team encouraged each employee to define what the purpose statement meant to them, and how they could bring it to life in their day-to-day work.

The purpose became the heart of the organization, the reason why it exists. Since the formation of the purpose, everything the company does has been linked to **"innovating to help everyone live well"**. Its strategy, values and employee proposition all come together to support the purpose.

The company's strategy is to reinforce and to reimagine — to build on its solid foundation and improve upon the things it already does well, so that it may get bigger and stronger. At the same time, to rethink what insurance could be, and to reshape the industry.

The five core values that underpin Prudential Singapore's culture — innovation, collaboration, trust, empowerment and accountability — guide the company's ways of working and interactions. Among the five values, innovation is the most significant value as the purpose requires employees to open their minds to possibilities, question assumptions to uncover new insights and come out with new solutions to emerging business and social problems.

For the purpose to be credible, fulfillment of it needs to start from within. Helping employees live well by creating an inclusive, empowered and collaborative work culture is a key part of the purpose work. To show the company's commitment to purpose, the performance of its leadership team is tied closely to the cultural health of the organization and measured by the extent to which each of the five core values — innovation, collaboration, accountability, empowerment and trust — is embedded in the ways of working. To this end, Prudential Singapore conducts a half-yearly survey on values to identify where the company is doing well, and the areas that need improvement, so the leadership team can develop strategies to make a positive cultural shift.

Ms. Parakkal said the company's performance assessment is underpinned by a very elaborate matrix, considering both business and culture outcomes. "This demonstrates to employees that we take our purpose and values very seriously. A purpose serves as a compass to everything we do. To do this, it must be aligned to strategy, values and the promise that we make to employees, customers and the community", said Ms. Parakkal.

ASSIMILATE

Prudential Singapore's leadership team does not see that its work ends with the launch of the purpose. A quick scan of the public literature available on the insurer's various initiatives is testimony to this. To understand the well-being of Singaporeans, Prudential Singapore commissioned a research programme called "Ready for 100: Preparing for Longevity in Singapore" which explores the challenges and opportunities of longer lives from four aspects of wellness: health, wealth, fulfilling careers and relationships. The insights from the research have inspired many conversations about longevity and guided Prudential Singapore's strategy, solutions and policies.

On the back of the research which shows that people want to work for longer to stay active and to save up for retirement, Prudential Singapore scrapped the retirement age from its HR policy in October 2018. Today, its employees are allowed to work for as long as they are able to perform. The company is of the opinion that there is a lot to gain from tapping the experience and knowledge of its more mature employees and it is committed to supporting them in extending their productive years by offering them re-skilling and up-skilling opportunities. This bold move was applauded by its employees and caught the attention of many, including the government and the media.

One person who was impressed by what he was reading was the current CEO, Mr. Dennis Tan, who joined Prudential Singapore in February 2020.

Mr. Tan shared, "News about Prudential scrapping its retirement age piqued my interest as it was a very progressive move and showed that the company values its employees for their experience. As I read more about Prudential's efforts to help Singaporeans live well for longer through its solutions and community initiatives, it became clear to me that its leadership team does not just focus on sales but drives a higher purpose".

Within the first couple of weeks in Prudential Singapore, Mr. Tan witnessed first-hand how the purpose is activated by the people of Prudential. Mr. Tan recalled, "As I interacted with my leadership team and various employees, I could sense and see the sheer passion in them as they explained their work and roles to me. Employees spoke about innovation and translating ideas into actions to help people live well. I see teams collaborating to find unique solutions. It was clear to me that the purpose is not just a paper exercise, or a slogan on the wall. As the CEO and an employee of Prudential Singapore, I am inspired by this purpose-driven culture".

ACTIVATE

In line with its purpose, Prudential Singapore is constantly innovating and breaking boundaries to introduce industry-first initiatives that help people to achieve overall well-being.

A noteworthy initiative is the launch of a cutting-edge, artificial intelligence-powered digital health app, "Pulse by Prudential", in April 2020. The app provides Singapore residents with round-the-clock access to healthcare services and real-time health information. It enables users to check their symptoms; conduct a digital health assessment to better understand future disease risks; and seek timely health advice, at any time and from anywhere. When Mr. Tan launched this app, he shared that the spread of COVID-19 created a greater sense of awareness and urgency to check symptoms when one is unwell, and to take better care of one's health and well-being. The launch of the app in Singapore was timely in light of the COVID-19 spread and the nation's circuit-breaker measures.

In addition to Pulse, Prudential Singapore implemented various initiatives to safeguard the health and wellness of its employees, customers, distributors, partners and the community amid the COVID-19 spread. At the onset of the pandemic, Prudential Singapore launched a S$1.5 million PRUCare package to provide complimentary COVID-19 cover and greater peace of mind to various groups during a very challenging period of time.

Under its PRUCare package, Prudential provided its customers and their immediate family members who were impacted by COVID-19 a quarantine cash benefit and daily hospitalization allowance for up to three months of hospitalization. These benefits were also made available to employees of Prudential's corporate and SME customers, its 1,400 employees and 5,000 financial consultants. In addition, the insurer also provided its existing SME customers the option to defer their premium payments for up to 3 months to better manage their cash flow and to ensure that there was no disruption to employees' coverage, so they can continue receiving the medical and hospitalization care they need.

Mr. Tan recounted, "Our PRUCare package was designed in line with our purpose. It is inclusive and supports our customers, employees, financial consultants and their families. As a life insurer with nearly a century of history in Singapore, we have the responsibility to stand by the community during this period of time".

For Prudential Singapore, ensuring it can continue to do business while keeping its employees, financial consultants and customers safe is key during the COVID-19 period. The insurer developed a remote selling tool in a record seven days at the height of the pandemic so its financial consultants can continue to meet the health and protection needs of its customers. The solution, called PRURemote Advice, is a video conferencing platform with an e-signature facility that enables its Agency to provide financial advisory and sell policies remotely without having to meet customers in person.

"As our financial consultants have always relied on face-to-face interactions, we needed to help them adjust and adapt fast during the COVID-19 period. Our customers still need their protection, and in fact, they require it more than ever with the escalating COVID-19 situation. They also need to be assured that their claims will be paid promptly even with 95% of our workforce working from home. I am very proud that the team acted with agility and came together very quickly to support our Agency and customers during a very challenging period of time", said Mr. Tan.

Mr. Tan also shared how PACS supported its employees with various wellness initiatives. With COVID-19 setting back travel plans and forcing everyone to stay at home, PACS decided to think out of the box to support its employees. The company offered to encash five leave days for all employees, in recognition that many would not be able to take leave for their yearly vacation.

When this request was tabled, Mr. Tan said his core leadership team unanimously supported it. The core leadership team also decided not to take advantage of the encashment scheme so as to not add additional financial burden to the company. Ms. Parakkal added, "The number of thank you messages and emails we received was unprecedented. We are very proud of this initiative and I think this is a testimony of the core leadership team putting purpose and people before profits".

CONCLUSION

What makes the purpose-led culture unique at Prudential Singapore is the bottom-up approach taken in developing it. The purpose statement, values and behaviors were co-created by the employees, resulting in a strong sense of ownership.

The purpose is also unique in that it puts innovation at the heart in a traditional industry not known for its agility and enterprise. And it is inclusive in that it is relevant to all of Prudential Singapore's stakeholders including the community, where the insurer works with groups such as vulnerable seniors and children through initiatives designed at advocating active ageing, tackling social isolation and promoting financial literacy.

The purpose-led culture helps every employee at Prudential Singapore focus on the long term, making work more meaningful and rewarding. Not surprisingly, the company has earned strong recognition for its efforts in promoting wellness and innovation through the many awards it has received.

The Prudential Singapore Charter, which focuses on the purpose and values, is depicted as follows.

Prudential Charter

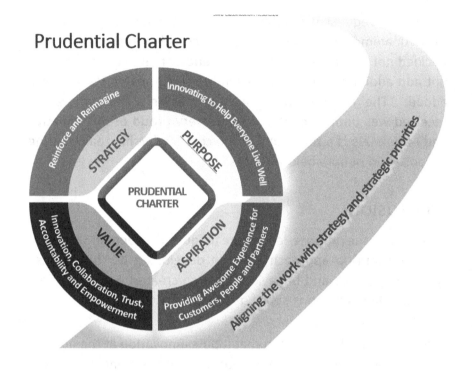

9. Red Hat: *Red Hat Exists to Promote Openness*

INTRODUCTION

When Finnish software engineer Linus Torvalds created a computer operating system that was open to all in 1991, he laid the foundation for a revolution that became known as open source computing. Open source software is software where the original source code is documented and made freely available to anyone for learning, redistribution, modification and improvement. This meant that for the first time in history, people from any company (or no company) from anywhere in the world could contribute to software development — their contribution would be pegged not to titles or positions but to the value of their contribution. What has resulted is a form of hyper-transparency.

Open source has been in Red Hat's DNA since its founding in 1993. It offered one of the earliest Linux operating system distributions; created the Fedora project (https://getfedora.org) for the development of free and open source software; and manages the opensource.com website that highlights the application of open-source philosophy to business, education, government, law, health and life. According to Mike Walker, global director of Open Innovation Labs at Red Hat, the characteristics found in the communities of open-source coding define the company's work culture and perspective. At Red Hat, open source is not just a technology but a way of thinking that extends beyond enterprise IT to domains such as culture, transparency, adaptability and collaboration.[1]

"Red Hat exists to promote openness — to be a champion for collaboration, sharing and transparency in the world. We're leaders in a movement that's bigger than ourselves. We work to defend software freedom, connect people and ideas, and show the world the power of the open source way". By connecting customers seeking open source solutions with the communities that create those solutions, Red Hat grew rapidly to become the first US$2 billion open source company in the world. It later expanded its business into new sectors including enterprise storage, container management, middleware, cloud computing and training. "Instead of being seen as an alternative choice or a cost-saving option, open source is now the new normal in enterprise technology... It is where innovation is happening and its enabling organizations to take a more agile approach to digital transformation", says Walker. Even as Red Hat acquired other companies to fuel its growth, it open-sourced its technology to further build out open source software solutions.[2] In July 2019, Red Hat was acquired by IBM for US$34 billion.

ARTICULATE

"At Red Hat, we believe openness unlocks the world's potential...
...to share knowledge and build upon each other's discoveries.
...to solve complex problems by bringing passionate people together to collaborate.
...to create communities where everyone is fully supported to use their voices and talents to contribute".

---

[1] https://sdtimes.com/os/red-hats-open-source-way/.
[2] https://sdtimes.com/os/red-hats-open-source-way/.

These words articulate Red Hat's purpose. Underlying this purpose is the belief that sharing is better, more productive and ultimately more enriching than hoarding, even though it wasn't always a popular view in the software industry.

But a statement of purpose wasn't something that existed from day one — it had to be crafted and articulated. According to DeLisa Alexander, Red Hat's Chief People Officer, one thing that was missing was "why Red Hat is here and what would be missing in the world if Red Hat weren't here.... We didn't have a common purpose to look up to and to be able to say, "Okay, this can guide us on how we make decisions". Once a company gets to a certain size and grows increasingly distant from the early days of its founders' daily involvement, the multiplicity of purposes can result in conflict and loss of a direction.

Instead of adopting a top-down approach where a handful of senior executives decided unilaterally on a purpose statement, the company introduced the concept of purpose to Red Hatters during one of its meetings. It then asked everyone to share a story about a time when they were really proud of being a Red Hatter. This process elicited 2,400 story submissions from out of 11,000 people at that time. Given that they had to write stories, not one-liners, this represented a very high participation rate.

To process 2,400 stories, Red Hat developed an open source programming language that could distil all the data into overarching themes. Once the program identified the themes, it became clear that certain functions had more affinity towards certain themes. Subsequently, each function was given specific themes and asked to think about a "why" statement or statement of purpose for itself. Despite initial doubts from a number of people, Red Hat proceeded with the exercise. As it was a truly ground-up process, it took the company a full year to articulate the statements that opened this section. But when the statements did come out, the response from Red Hatters was overwhelmingly positive because they were involved all the way and thus developed a stake in it.

The creation of its mission statement — "To be the catalyst in communities of customers, contributors, and partners creating better technology the open source way" — was a similarly open and collaborative effort. In 2009, Red Hat gathered feedback from all employees to ensure it represented the entire company and to stay within Red Hat's open source vision.

Says DP van Leeuwen, Senior Vice President and General Manager for Red Hat Asia Pacific and Japan:

> "It is all about sharing and being open about sharing. It is contrary to most successful business models, where it's all about intellectual property, owning the idea and protecting that idea. It's about sharing the idea and not wanting to own it but letting somebody else build upon it. It's not about ownership — it's about creation and creativity.
>
> It doesn't matter who you are, where you are, what you studied or what your background is. If you have a good idea, then you should have a platform to share the idea. And if you share the idea, somebody else should have the opportunity to pick it up and to evolve on it, or to do something entirely different with it. Just put it to good use. This is, I think, how technology and innovation have grown exponentially. This exponential growth that we are seeing right now in digital disruption is primarily driven through open source, because everybody has access to the technology".

Red Hat's open philosophy extends even to its competitors. That is, its competitors have complete access to all its software design and are free to make better versions of the software if they choose to do so.

ASSIMILATE

Open source communities expect to have the opportunity to participate immediately and without regard for titles, tenure or dues. Furthermore, they expect to have open access to the entire software development process (including bugs) as well as transparency regarding decisions made by the company. As Red Hat has actively participated in, contributed to and hired from many open source communities, it was almost inevitable that its culture would assimilate the transparency and collaboration that characterize these communities. Over time, Red Hat learned that many of the ways open source communities function are also effective approaches to running its business.[3]

Red Hat's open source ethos and way of developing software has resulted in Red Hatters having values that are quite different from what might be seen and experienced in more traditional hierarchical organizations. But it doesn't come naturally to many people. A lot of Red Hat's employees had worked previously in traditional environments where they were rewarded for making quick top-down decisions and then rolling change management out; the company recognizes that these new employees might need help in making the transition.

All new hires are schooled in the Red Hat multiplier, which are five ways of working together that multiply individual efforts and innovation. These five ways are "connection", "trust", "transparency", "collaboration" and "meritocracy". It also has manager training

---

[3] https://thefutureorganization.com/red-hat-culture-open-leadership/.

that helps those who are in people management roles to understand what it is like to manage and what the company expects from Red Hat managers. In addition, Red Hat has accelerated leadership development programs, which are highly intense programs that help people take their leadership from one level of mastery to a much higher level, focusing on open leadership. Open leadership is not restricted to those in formal leadership positions — every Red Hatter has the responsibility to lead. The open leadership mindset is one that believes in everyone having the untapped potential to learn and grow. It involves establishing the conditions that allow people to extend themselves and grow into that potential. In addition, open leadership means putting the organization and the community over self — the company's leaders believe that everyone wins when people do that versus focusing on achieving on individual goals.[4] In Red Hat's Asian operations, van Leeuwen equates open leadership with facilitation:

> "My role in Asia Pacific is just facilitating. If I can continue to facilitate, then the people we're hiring can be their personal best in whatever they do, and have a platform for being listened to and to develop ideas. That's my role. In a traditional company, you would expect somebody in my position to be directive and to tell others what to do and be really top-down. This is really the culture that we've been building that people love".

In addition to training, a seemingly innocuous communication tool called memo-list has played a significant part in embedding transparency and collaboration in Red Hat's culture. Memo-list is an internal email list that serves as a companywide forum for discussions on any topic. Memo-list cuts through the hierarchy that discourages sharing and ideation by allowing all associates direct access to everyone in the company — including the CEO. Their online messages are visible to anyone who chooses to be on the

---

[4] https://thefutureorganization.com/red-hat-culture-open-leadership/.

list. Among other topics, memo-list has facilitated debates about where Red Hat is headed as a company, what technologies are used internally and changes to benefit policies.

To align its internal decision-making and project leadership with open source principles, Red Hat launched its Open Decision Framework — a collection of best practices — in 2012. It released the framework publicly in 2016 on GitHub to spur collaboration and transparency among other organizations. Developed through open collaboration by Red Hatters from around the world, the framework offers practical steps to help teams collaborate with each other, identify and engage stakeholders, manage competing needs and priorities, communicate trade-offs and business require-ments, and improve decision-making. It relies on five open source principles:

1. Open exchange
2. Participation
3. Meritocracy
4. Community
5. Release early, release often

Nonetheless, while having an open culture has many benefits, not everyone knows how to have a high-stakes conversation in a way that is open yet productive. To create a culture where difficult con-versations aren't so difficult, Red Hat once again drew from its roots in the open source world, where having candid conversations is the norm. It subsequently enshrined three behaviors, which are aimed at creating a safe environment in which everyone feels com-fortable having difficult conversations:

1. Show appreciation
2. Open up (to hear what people say)
3. Be inclusive early and often

These practices have helped to create a vibrant feedback loop within the company where open and honest feedback is shared, thus improving the chances that issues are being addressed, and more quickly.[5]

Red Hat's open culture sometimes means that decisions take longer to be made, as more time is spent listening to all the inputs and weighing all the options. Nonetheless, as van Leeuwen points out, Red Hat's decision-making process is anchored in meritocracy and not in democracy:

> "Meritocracy is the basis of open source. It is about the best idea wins and not about the majority deciding what is best. For example, if the customer needs a feature or function in our product, we will take those requests and post them on a worldwide forum in the open source community. If what we call the upstream community sees that these requests make sense, we'll embed them in the solution".

When IBM acquired Red Hat in 2019, it co-established with Red Hat a common set of ground rules, but kept both companies organizationally separate:

> "We work very, very, closely with them — I have IBM meetings and calls on a daily basis. But when we don't see eye to eye, or when there is ambiguity, we always fall back on our Red Hat culture. We protect our culture in that sense very heavily".

The benefits of Red Hat's open culture are reflected in its employee engagement metrics, which outperform those of many of its peer companies. For example, it performed above the technology-company benchmark for each of the seven questions

---

[5] Whitehurst, 2015.

from its survey for which external standards were available. A notable example is that almost 85% of Red Hatters indicated feeling comfortable being themselves at work, compared with 76% for benchmark companies.

ACTIVATE

Red Hat has started various corporate social responsibility (CSR) initiatives in Asia. But it is the company's response to the COVID-19 crisis in Asia that truly shows how its purpose is activated, said van Leeuwen:

> "Healthcare could tremendously benefit from open source. To find the cure for COVID, everybody can go off in isolation to try to fix and find the solution, and financially benefit from it or use the fact that the research is so expensive, and say "Okay, we can't share it. This has to be our own intellectual property, and now we will introduce medication and we will make billions out of a vaccine that the whole world is going to need". That's one way — the traditional way— of how healthcare is approaching issues in the world. Our way of approaching it is, "Okay let's share everybody's research. Let's make it public between doctors and specialists and virologists who understand how these things work". And use this to very quickly — because this is the exponential innovation that happens when you look at each other's ideas and each other's work — eliminate the bad stuff, build on the good stuff which dramatically increases the speed to delivery. Ultimately, you have the solution right where you can benefit from it. You can still find ways of making money — it's just not on protecting an intellectual property so that you prevent other people from benefitting from it".

In 2020, Red Hat helped the Singapore government to launch Open Trace, a project to open source the code of the TraceTogether app, which is used to track the contacts of infected people in the fight against the COVID-19 virus. It has the distinction of being the world's first contact tracing app. Developed in an eight-week sprint, TraceTogether has been downloaded by over a million users (or about 1 in 5 residents in Singapore) to support Singapore's contact tracing operations. Since its launch, the Singapore government has received many requests to replicate TraceTogether internationally.

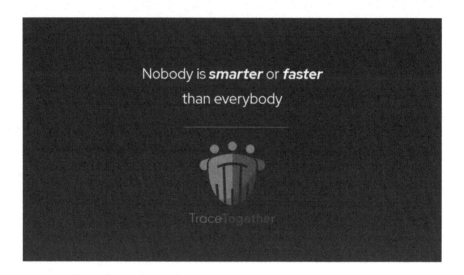

Red Hat's efforts to cultivate an open, diverse and inclusive environment includes the setting up of its PRIDE chapter in Singapore, its first in the region. These efforts also extend beyond the company's parameters to include the open source and other communities in the Asia-Pacific region. For example, it has set up a Women's Leadership Council in Korea; the next chapter is being set up in Singapore. van Leeuwen is himself a mentor in the mentoring program of the NGO Protégé, which aims to promote women leaders.

CONCLUSION

Red Hat was founded on the belief that open source would democratize software development and confer immense benefits to all participants in the wider community. This ethos quickly developed into a higher purpose that defines what the company stands for, shapes the behavior of people who work at the company, and catalyzes truly collaborative partnerships with external stakeholders for social impact. In a business world that is placing greater emphasis on openness, transparency and diversity, Red Hat's purpose-led journey offers an inspiration.

REFERENCES

Morgan, J. (2019). A look at Red Hat's culture: How they use open leadership, creating meaning at work, dealing with change, and much more. Available at: https://thefutureorganization.com/red-hat-culture-open-leadership/.
Whitehurst, J. (2015). Create a culture where difficult conversations aren't so hard. *Harvard Business Review*.

10. Royal DSM N.V. (DSM): Creating Brighter Lives for All

INTRODUCTION

The company that the world knows as DSM started as Dutch State Mines in 1902. In the 1980s, its managing board made the call that coal would not be a sustainable business in the long run. Thereafter, it moved out of coal and into bulk petro- and specialty chemicals. Subsequently, through M&As and divestments, the company also got out of bulk chemicals and transitioned to businesses that would ensure societal, environmental and its own sustainability.

Today, DSM is a global purpose-led and performance-driven company specializing in nutrition, health and sustainable living. Its purpose is to "**create brighter lives for all**" by using its scientific and innovation expertise and resources to tackle some of the world's greatest challenges, and to create value for customers, shareholders, employees and society at large as it does so. Underlying this purpose is the belief that people, the planet and profit are equally important.

In March 2019, DSM announced its intention to be one of the most environmentally friendly producers in the coating resins industry and the market-leading supplier of sustainable solutions. So committed is DSM to "creating brighter lives for all" that its corporate strategy is aligned with five of the United Nations Sustainable Development Goals (SDGs):

2 — zero hunger,
3 — good health and well-being,
7 — affordable and clean energy,
12 — responsible consumption and production and
13 — climate action.

ARTICULATE

More than a decade ago, it was generally believed that businesses could either achieve profit or improve the planet, but not both. DSM, on the other hand, subscribes to the philosophy that good financial performance and doing well for the world are not mutually exclusive to each other. In fact, they will have to go hand in hand or companies will lose their license to operate. "We cannot be successful, nor even call ourselves successful, in a society that fails", according to Feike Sijbesma, Honorary Chairman of DSM.

DSM's leaders believe that the huge growth in the impact that companies have had in the last 70 years brings with it greater responsibility. They also believe that companies, with their technological expertise and capacity for innovation, can provide answers to the world's greatest challenges. Last, they believe that companies should deliver value not just to customers and employees, but to the world's communities and the individuals who live in them.

According to Pieter Nuboer, Chief Operating Officer, DSM-ERBER, DSM's purpose of "creating brighter lives for all" came out of the company's "Brighter Science. Brighter Living" positioning as a strategic intent:

> "Creating brighter lives for generations today and those to come, involved connecting our two elements — we have a material science

element, and a life science element. It's also about finding the X factor in the innovation power between those two, to come up with innovations that will have a meaningful impact on people and on the planet".

Having a purpose means having a totally different mindset. In this mindset, purpose drives performance and results. Among DSM employees, the company's name has even assumed a new meaning in recent years: "Doing Something Meaningful".

What makes DSM unique is that purpose is integral to strategy. The company's strategy marries its purpose with global megatrends and the UN Sustainable Development Goals to create growth opportunities in the focal domains of nutrition and health, climate and energy, and resources and circularity.[1] A strategy in which purpose plays a driving role ensures that purpose provides the 'North Star' that guides the company's major decisions and actions. Its *Improve-Enable-Advocate* framework offers an actionable framework that marries purpose with strategy:

1. *Improve*: Reducing the impact of its operations (e.g. reducing emissions) can help DSM to lower costs and risks and achieve greater sustainability.

---

[1] Two examples of this strategy are provided in the segment on "ACTIVATE".

2. *Enable*: Enabling its customers to deliver sustainable and healthy solutions can spur growth in innovative sustainable solutions.
3. *Advocate*: Advocating for a more sustainable business environment can create higher engagement among its employees, shareholders and society.

This purpose-led, performance-driven strategy has resulted in several awards for DSM: Dow Jones Sustainability Index, 100 World's Most Sustainable Corporations, MSCI, Fortune Magazine's "Change the World".

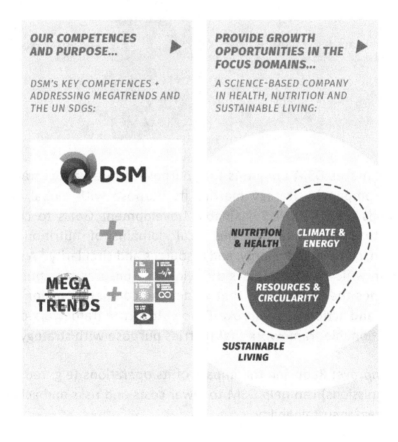

ASSIMILATE

DSM achieves its purpose through its way of working (i.e. its culture and people). At the company, purpose is built on the foundation of an inclusive culture. It is a culture where employees are made to feel safe and have a voice at the table, so that people feel they are included and heard. This creates a sense of ownership over the company's journey towards achieving a shared purpose.[2]

Diversity is also extremely important. At DSM, diversity is rapidly moving beyond traditional definitions, as Nuboer explains:

> "It is no longer just about gender or nationality. You want to really build the culture where you create diversity of thought, and where you consciously develop and hire for complementary skills that make teams complete, whether that's more towards the interpersonal, the strategic or the tactical domain. Diversity of thought on top of the traditional parameters is paramount, particularly given the monumental tasks facing the world. You need bright ideas and for that, you need great inclusiveness and great diversity of thought".

In other words, exceptional diversity of thought would give DSM the intellectual prowess it needs to address the monumental societal challenges, guided by its purpose.

DSM's strong culture of Safety, Health and Environment (SHE) also helps to systematically embed its purpose throughout the organization. Each product goes through a rigorous Life Cycle Analysis (LCA) so that its environmental and social impact is known. In

---

[2] https://www.accenture.com/nl-en/blogs/insights/how-could-dsm-transform-so-successfully-into-a-purpose-driven-business.

addition, it uses renewable energy sources such as POET-DSM advanced biofuels and high-performance solar panels to manufacture its products. The company also conducts regular sustainability audits according to the guidelines of the Global Reporting Initiative.[3]

Recruiting the right people and socializing them also plays a part in assimilating purpose. Nuboer looks for leadership purpose in new hires — this is especially true for talent and roles that will eventually shape organizational health. He deliberately looks beyond their ability to deliver results and takes into account their potential to lead for purpose: "Does the individual speak the language of things, or the language of ideas? Does the individual think in terms of consequences of the past, or in terms of consequences of the future"?

At DSM, socialization is a systematic, ongoing process that starts from day one. It focuses on the imperative to enhance the company's operational impact by further improving safety, decreasing emissions and stepping up the use of renewable energy. Nuboer and his team constantly ask themselves how they can improve their footprint and enable their customers to do the same through applications, innovation and new products. In addition, they constantly ask themselves what alliances they could be shaping to advocate the need for action and ensure delivery on the UN SDGs.

To keep track of its progress in embedding purpose, DSM uses the findings from its annual employment engagement survey (EES). These findings consistently show that DSM employees feel that this is a company where safety and sustainability are prioritized. Nonetheless, the challenge of socializing purpose will always be a

---

[3] https://www.businesstimes.com.sg/hub/aces-awards-2018/the-green-factor-in-success.

work in progress and one that is not unique to DSM. Nuboer sees the challenge in this way:

"How do we make this relevant across all work levels, both top-down and bottom-up? Global, regional and local? When the mind-set is "This is my job, I need to pay my bills", how can you inject that relevance there about improving, enabling, and advocating? How do you get to institutionalize purpose across the organization"?

According to him, the key is to continuously socialize the "why" and achieve transformational impact beyond traditional CSR. DSM's engagement surveys show that both efforts have resonated well with its employees over a longer period of time.

ACTIVATE

DSM has long believed that it needs to work side by side with part-ners including governments, international organizations, industry bodies, peers and even competitors to activate and amplify its purpose of "creating brighter lives for all". This belief is based on the recognition that DSM can punch above its weight by bringing the brightest minds together to address the world's big issues. This partnership mindset is reflected in Nuboer's words:

> "Scientific expertise is not exclusive to DSM. It's about really con-necting industries and consumers with science for there to be an impact. It does not start with what percentage share of the inno-vation we need… This is about science that needs to be pro-moted and adopted for societal purpose".

DSM's leaders believe that meaningful change can be brought about by enabling its customers and partners to deliver sustainable and healthy solutions for the planet and society. Another is by advocating for the future that it believes in and fully accepting its responsibilities as a social citizen. Both "enabling" and "advocating" are codified as two of the three "DSM actions" (the other being "improving").

DSM's Asia Pacific headquarters in Singapore has started three initiatives that involve "enabling" and "advocating". According to Nuboer, these strategic initiatives can help the company and its employees transcend the more "transactional" mindset in Asia, which tends to focus on sales, marketing and short-term goals.

Bright Science Hub

Asia is facing daunting environmental challenges — "including those related to unsustainable resource management and natural resource depletion, ecosystem degradation and biodiversity loss, pollution and waste, and climate change" (ESCAP, p. 1) — that threaten the region's prosperity and social development.[4] What has DSM Asia Pacific done to address these challenges?

In November 2019, DSM partnered with Padang & Co (an innovation accelerator) to launch the Bright Science Hub. The initiative aims to foster the co-creation of breakthrough solutions to attain the following five SDGs for Asia: 2 (Zero hunger), 3 (Good health and well-being), 7 (Affordable and clean energy), 12 (Responsible production and consumption) and 13 (Climate Action).

The hub focuses on promoting equitable access to healthy food and nutrition, enabling the sustainable production of diversified proteins and food waste reduction, while promoting low-carbon technologies. It does so by providing start-ups, teams from DSM's collaborations and other entities with a collaborative workspace as

---

[4] ESCAP (2018). Key environment issues, trends and challenges in the Asia-Pacific region. Available at https://www.unescap.org/sites/default/files/CED5_1E_0.pdf.

well as access to DSM's ecosystem, networks, scientific expertise and laboratories (for the prototyping and development of nutritional products). In addition, it hosts events to foster learning and connections, and programs to build capabilities.

While the hub wasn't ostensibly set up with the purpose to make DSM's people socialize, it has already had that effect. By providing them with a platform to interact (both formally and informally) with hub tenants such as aquaculture incubators, the company is enabling DSM employees to see and experience shared purpose in action.

Despite the disruptions caused by COVID-19, DSM has already started to see compelling evidence of the power of greater connectivity with multiple stakeholders across relevant value chains. For example, the Smart Farm initiative brings together feed mills, farms, technology companies and start-ups to gather the data that are needed to achieve optimized yields and emissions through precision nutrition. The company has also entered into a strategic partnership with the US Soybean Export Council.

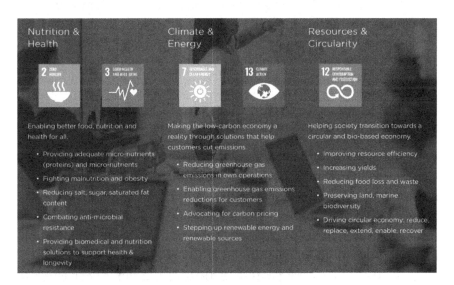

The Cultiv@te Initiative ("Enable")

In 2020, DSM signed a letter of intent to became a strategic partner of the UNDP Global Centre for Technology Innovation & Sustainable Development (GCTISD) for its Cultiv@te initiative in Asia. Cultiv@te functions as a platform for multi-country thematic partnerships — called "Co-Labs" — where start-ups, government agencies, companies and researchers come together to address the most pressing development challenges. DSM's focus here again is on the value-chain transformation of aquaculture and livestock in Asia. Ultimately, its efforts will help the stakeholders contribute to the SDGs through scientifically proven precision nutrition solutions.

The Cultiv@te Initiative is one that Nuboer is passionate about, especially as it represents an opportunity to take greater control of its purpose agenda in Asia and rely less on global initiatives:

> "The value chain for global production of marine agriculture products — you're talking for example about prawns, tilapia and catfish, etc. — approximately 90% comes from Asia, including China. It's a massive industry where emissions control or the use of precision nutrition, I would argue, is increasingly on the radar. But there is a lot more work to be done in adopting the science and creating the impacts that are needed in relation to the sustainable development goals".

Sustainability Program with SMU ("Advocate")

DSM and Singapore Management University (SMU) are in a partnership that will provide experimental learning opportunities for SMU students through the university's award-winning SMU-X pedagogy. Out of two credit-bearing learning opportunties, one will focus on sustainability at large while another will focus on nutrition improvement. Both will be offered at the Lee Kong Chian School of Business (LKBCS), starting in the 2020–2021 academic year. Nuboer strongly believes that universities need to do a lot more to promote and embed the strategic relevance of sustainability:

> *Anecdotally, in the events where we talk to MBA students due to graduate, I once asked a group of five "Tell me a bit more about this topic", and I got a bit of a glare, like "What is he going on about"? I said, "It is a living topic, does it bother you at all"? What they said when I got them to talk will always be stuck in my mind. I got a couple of remarks saying "Well, it's not a very popular course". Course? Is it a course? And "I first need to get a job and pay back my student loan". Of course, very relevant, I get it, and I see in there a lot of opportunity to socialize more the big "why". Because the need is so pressing, and we are past midnight".*

CONCLUSION

DSM's purpose was born out of its transformational journey to be a sustainable organization that also creates sustainable solutions for some of the world's challenges. Its journey so far offers some valuable lessons to other organizations that are thinking about how to articulate, assimilate and activate their purpose.

First, DSM's integration of purpose with corporate strategy at the global level ensures that purpose drives performance and vice versa. For example, by improving the impact of its own operations, enabling sustainable solutions for its customers and advocating sustainable business, DSM can grow faster and reduce its cost and risk profile. The mutual reinforcement of purpose and performance is what makes the purpose itself sustainable: without tangible business results, the resources required to activate its purpose and make it socially impactful will dry up. In turn, performance validates purpose and empowers it to continue setting the scope for further business growth and evolution.

Another important contribution that DSM makes to the conversation on purpose is the importance it places on diversity when assimilating purpose. At first glance, diversity may appear to have little to do with purpose. But when looked at more deeply, diversity — particularly in thought and skills — gives DSM access to the wider array of intellectual talent that is needed to address the increasingly complex social and environmental problems in ways that also drive performance. Diversity gets measured in its employment engagement survey, and "what gets measured, gets done".

DSM's purpose-led journey in Asia may be relatively new. But its investment in ground-up, "Asia-first" initiatives makes it a model for showing how a global purpose can be translated into local and regional action. The results of these initiatives bear watching.

11. Siemens AG (Siemens): *Creating Environments that Care*

INTRODUCTION

More than 170 years ago, Siemens was founded on an idea that was ahead of its time: A company should not focus on only maximizing profits. It should also serve society with its technologies and products and its employment practices. The company's founder, Werner von Siemens, said categorically that he would not sell the future of the company for instant profit. This ethos is still very much alive today. According to Joe Kaeser, President and CEO of Siemens AG, "serving society while doing successful and sustainable business is at the heart of Siemens's strategy. It's our company's ultimate purpose". This purpose is translated into three dictums:

"We serve society".
"We create value for all stakeholders".
"We make real what matters".

Headquartered in Munich, Germany, Siemens is today a technology giant powerhouse that stands for engineering excellence, innovation, quality, reliability and internationality. The principal divisions of the company are Digital Industries, Smart Infrastructure, Energy, Healthcare and Mobility. The company is a component of the Euro Stoxx 50 stock market index. Siemens and its subsidiaries employ approximately 385,000 people worldwide and reported global revenue of around €87 billion in 2019.

As a leading global technology company, Siemens responds to global megatrends such as digital transformation, globalization, urbanization, demographic change and climate change and provides solutions in the areas of electrification, automation and digitalization.

As part of its new sustainable development agenda, Siemens aims to end poverty, protect the planet and ensure prosperity by providing access to clean and affordable energy solutions, creating smart and liveable cities, and providing access to innovative healthcare systems. In doing so, Siemens aligns itself with the goals of the UN's 2030 Agenda for Sustainable Development. The company's commitment to sustainability is widely recognized in numerous significant ratings and rankings, including the Dow Jones Sustainability Indices, Corporate Knights, Clean200 and CDP.

Smart Infrastructure

Siemens has a diverse range of businesses — each dovetails the overarching corporate purpose with its specific expertise and portfolio. This chapter focuses on the company's Smart Infrastructure business, which is focused on making the world a more connected and "caring" place (i.e. where resources are valued, where impact on the world is considered, where sustainable energy is delivered reliably and efficiently). It does this by offering a range of solutions from physical products, components and systems to connected, cloud-based digital offerings and a combination of advisory and digital services. "**Creating environments that care**" is its purpose.

ARTICULATE

Smart Infrastructure was formed in April 2019 by bringing together business units from Building Technologies, Energy Management and Digital Factory under the same roof. The Smart

Infrastructure business invariably ended up with a customer base that encompassed the entire community. The need to serve such a wide spectrum of stakeholders called for a unifying purpose that could coalesce the different ideologies and cultures into one. As Elangovan Karuppiah, CEO, Regional Solutions and Services, Middle East/Asia Pacific describes:

> "Some of the units were focused on the product businesses, so they sell through third-party channels like indirect sellers and local system integrators and so on. We had a large part of the Building Technologies unit that was embedded in each and every country — it was very localized in its operations, bringing their services to the customer at their doorstep. Bringing the products business, systems business and solutions business together was one big challenge".

Over the years, individual divisions and operating companies within Siemens were encouraged to craft their own motto — a "sub-purpose" as it were — from the three dictums. This welcoming environment provided the Smart Infrastructure group with the opportunity to create its "Creating environments that care" motto, which articulates its intent to address infrastructure challenges, contribute to sustainable development and create the best possible environments for people to live and work — by leveraging the combined strengths of three different groups of people. True to its emphasis on *care*, the motto was deliberately the outcome of a consultative process that involved both the leadership team and the staff.

To quantitatively measure its social impact around multiple dimensions, such as driving economic growth, enabling job creation and skills, advancing innovation, sustaining the environment, improving quality of life and improving societal inclusion, Siemens developed the ®**Business to Society** methodology. The methodology also allows the company to understand its contribution towards the UN

Agenda for Sustainable Development as well as to measure Siemens' overall social impact on a project, on a country or global level.

In addition, Siemens participates in the Dow Jones Sustainability Index every year to emphasize internally and externally that it is committed to ensuring sustainability in its businesses, so that it can survive up to 200 years after its founding.

ASSIMILATE

Siemens's ethos of "care" is enshrined as one of the four pillars of its Leadership Compass, a formal set of four values by which people at Siemens navigate their business decisions. Since its inception in 2019, the Leadership Compass has acted as a moral compass and helped to embed purpose by making the caring of customers, society, the environment and fellow employees a top priority. Each of the four elements of the Compass spells out specific and measurable behaviors, actions and attitudes that translate into "care" for different stakeholders. The Leadership Compass was brought together by Siemens's most senior leaders, together with Human Resources and Communications. Each leader gave input on its design, incorporating what is most important to them and to their people.

To promote the internalization of the four values of "caring", the company has made the Compass an integral part of its performance review and hiring process. During performance reviews, employees are assessed on how well they have (1) engaged their teams, customers and other employees, (2) empowered their teams, (3) focused on customers, solutions and agility and (4) cared for their teams, customers, society, environment and one another. In addition, the Compass is a key part of hiring and succession planning, as candidates undergo an assessment based on the four elements.

As Smart Infrastructure is a very young organization within a centuries-old company, its culture is still in an evolving and formative stage. One of the biggest challenges Smart Infrastructure faced was how to coalesce the different cultures in the Building Technologies, Energy Management and Digital Factory business units into *one* purpose-driven company culture. The Leadership Compass facilitates the assimilation of purpose by giving teams the flexibility to decide which of the elements under the four values to emphasize for their own business unit.

Another key challenge has to do with making these values come to life, so that they are not just words on a slide. To address this challenge, Smart Infrastructure selected a pilot group of leaders who embodies the values in the Leadership Compass to act as amplifiers. These leaders will have the responsibility of "walking the walk" and "talking the talk" so that the principles behind the compass are manifested and experienced.

To ensure deeper and broader assimilation of its purpose within its cultural fabric, the company is also developing new toolkits to provide guidance and best-practice examples on how to better engage, empower, focus and care. Ongoing leadership dialogues and fireside chats between company leaders and employees also aid in the assimilation of purpose.

The COVID-19 pandemic and the associated lockdowns inspired the launch of a weekly online TV show. Aptly named KeepCaring TV, the show acts as a forum for the discussion of salient topics ranging from personal well-being to change management. During these unprecedented times, KeepCaring TV has managed to encourage dialogue and to allow company leaders to have difficult conversations about challenging issues that confront their team members and customers. The themes of the show included vulnerability, trust and the acceptance of imperfection. The show's relaxed and unscripted format enables employees to see the people behind the names and job titles and to discuss these themes openly with one another and the audience. Some of the company's most senior leaders have let employees into their personal space in an unscripted conversational environment, encouraging colleagues to ask questions that they might not have had the courage to ask before. During a time when everyone was steering their lives through a global pandemic, the company's leaders opened up and shared personal experiences and feelings that helped employees to relate to them more personally. The leaders' candid comments in turn acted as an invitation to employees to express sentiments that had not been commonly expressed before. KeepCaring TV enabled employees to post responses to the episode on the medium's chat function. This regularly resulted in hundreds of comments being left on the episodes, including over 1000 repeat views of a recording.

ACTIVATE

Siemens Smart Infrastructure activates its "sub-purpose" of "Creating environments that care" in three strategic areas:

a. Smart buildings

This focal area is concerned with the question of how to turn what are essentially inanimate, silent and passive structures into living environments that can interact with their occupants, learn from them and ultimately adapt to their changing needs. One recent use case is the project for Taipei Veterans General Hospital (TVGH).

Smart Infrastructure's relationship with TVGH started in 2009 when it worked on TVGH's Medical Science & Technology Building (MSTB) upgrading project. MSTB is a multifunctional facility offering research services ranging from basic science to clinical medicine and testing.

There, the Siemens team used the latest digital technologies and the power of data to enhance air quality and energy efficiency, thus providing a more conducive environment for recuperating patients.

To enable MSTB to enhance its patient experience, Smart Infrastructure leveraged its expertise in HVAC (heating, ventilation and air conditioning) control to provide stable and precise airflow control for critical environments, thereby safeguarding patients and hospital staff. To help MSTB achieve its sustainability goals, the company created a physical environment where patient-centric medical/research excellence can be pursued in an energy-saving environment. It also provided new technologies that enabled data-driven services to enhance energy efficiency, optimize indoor air quality and comfort.

"As HVAC system plays a critical role in hospitals and accounts for a large proportion of energy use, Siemens's building technologies, precision controls and services really help us to reduce operating costs and increase the efficiency of our investments", said

Mr. Zhong, Zhao-An, Supervisor of the Engineering Department at TVGH.

With the company's help, MSTB became the first medical building in Taiwan to meet the requirements of Good Clinical Practice (GCP), Good Laboratory Practice (GLP) and Biosafety Level 2–3 (BL2-BL3) in Taiwan.

b. Smart grids

This focal area is focused on paving the way for sustainable energy environments by applying the Internet of Energy and data-driven technologies. In a fast-developing country such as Vietnam, the need for energy is rapidly growing. To meet this demand in a sustainable manner, the country needs to increase the percentage of renewable energy in its energy generation (among other things). Hence, the Vietnamese government has set a target of developing 18 gigawatts of solar and wind generating capacity by 2030. Siemens is supporting the achievement of this national goal by helping Vietnam's Trung Nam Group with its solar energy project.

Trung Nam's mission of "Sustainable investment — building up the future" and their commitment to innovative energy solutions mirror Smart Infrastructure's purpose of "creating environments that care". Smart Infrastructure's relationship with Trung Nam started in 2014 when the latter was seeking innovative solutions for its hydropower plants. When Trung Nam wanted to invest in a solar power plant within its wind farm area, Smart Infrastructure offered its expertise at a very early stage and proposed a design concept.

With significant savings in carbon emissions as the end goal, Smart Infrastructure helped Trung Nam to analyze the power plant's efficiency, calculate solar energy harvesting and provide domain know-how regarding new photovoltaic technology. When it was operational in 2019, Trung Nam's solar farm became the largest in Vietnam, supplying approximately 200,000 households with electricity and potentially saving about 250,000 tons of carbon dioxide.

c. Financing tomorrow's infrastructure

This focal area combines technology and domain expertise to develop the smart infrastructure as well as improve the energy ecosystems and building technologies that are key to transforming cities and industries. In rural India, securing reliable power supply has been a big challenge for thousands of villages. For some, power outage can occur for more than 12 hours a day, so providing a reliable power supply to these villages is crucial.

In 2019, the Government of India approached one of its renowned universities to take the lead in addressing this pressing and perennial issue. Recognizing the complexity of the solution, the university approached Smart Infrastructure on account of its technical expertise. This unique tripartite partnership enables the exchange of knowledge that could lead to a solution with the potential to address rural India's biggest challenge.

Leveraging Siemens' expertise in decarbonization, decentralization and digitalization, the collaboration will enable the creation of a sustainable and scalable smart microgrid solution that ensures carbon-free and reliable power supply, while providing villagers with new opportunities for revenue generation. Thanks to this initiative, Indian villagers can now already sell cattle dung to an NGO to earn extra income. The cattle dung is then used in a biomass plant to provide clean energy back to the villagers. Any residual ash is returned to the villagers for use as fertilizer, as their main source of income is from agriculture. This represents a win–win–win outcome for all the parties involved.

As Elangovan recounts, this initiative came about because of Smart Infrastructure's ongoing conversations with local NGOs in India:

> "We started to discuss with local NGOs that were caring for the villagers in that area who faced electricity disruptions regularly. They told us "Hey, can't you guys look on a larger scale? Besides doing upgrades at the university to improve their efficiency, can't you harness some of this to support the villagers? We are bringing to life a project which has the potential to help so many more of the underserved in society".

COVID-19

Like all the companies featured in this book, Siemens gave a purpose-led response to the COVID-19 pandemic. When the Singapore government designated several hotels in Singapore as quarantine facilities for COVID-19 patients, one of these hotels approached Siemens for help to find a solution on how to isolate the infected people. Smart Infrastructure provided advisory services on how to manage air flow and circulation to reduce the risks of the spread of the virus. To help the hotel reduce its operating costs at a time when hotel occupancy had taken a big hit, Smart Infrastructure installed new flow meters and sensors to optimize the flow of their pumps and reap energy savings.

In addition, Siemens was asked to help the underprivileged and the migrant workers in Singapore who were affected by the crisis. So, it organized a donation drive among its employees to raise funds for two NGOs, Food from the Heart and HealthServe. The funds raised would provide underprivileged school students and their families with food rations as well as medical care and social assistance to migrant workers.

CONCLUSION

Translating corporate purpose from the global HQ level to the country or business unit level is always going to present a major challenge. Siemens Smart Infrastructure is a good example of an organization within a multinational conglomerate that has achieved some early success in articulating, assimilating and activating its own purpose — while staying broadly aligned with the parent company's overarching purpose. It has managed to do so largely through its flexible implementation of the Leadership Compass. By activating its purpose in its three focal areas (i.e. Smart Buildings, Smart Grids, Building Tomorrow's Infrastructure), Smart Infrastructure has been able to ensure that its purpose is aligned with its strategy and stakeholder needs. Even though the COVID-19 pandemic has brought unprecedented challenges, it has also catalyzed the creation of initiatives such as KeepCaring TV that reinforces the company's purpose and values. Smart Infrastructure's journey thus far shows that being new and being part of a global conglomerate need not be impediments.

12. Tata Group (Tata): *Improving Communities through Long Term Stakeholder Value Creation*

INTRODUCTION

Founded by Jamsetji Nusserwanji Tata in 1868, the Tata group is a global enterprise headquartered in Mumbai, India, and one of India's oldest business empires. Popularly known as the "salt to software" conglomerate, it operates in several primary business sectors including steel, chemicals, automobiles, consumer products, energy, information systems, Airlines, Hotels, services and more. The group has a presence in more than 100 countries across six continents, employing over 720,000 people. Each Tata company or enterprise operates independently under the guidance and supervision of its own board of directors. Tata Sons is the principal holding and promoter company of the group. Sixty-six percent of the equity share capital of Tata Sons is held by philanthropic trusts that support non-governmental organizations working in the fields of education, livelihood generation, health, art, culture and many more social welfare initiatives. In 2018–2019, the revenue of Tata companies, taken together, was $113.0 billion (INR 792,710 crore).

Tata's 151 years of existence is closely intertwined with the history of Indian industry. It stays relevant even to this day because for the man on the streets of India, the Tata brand is associated with "trust". Furthermore, Jamsetji Tata is the only businessman to appear on the currency of a country. For the 175th birth anniversary of Jamsetji Tata in the year 2015, the Prime Minister of India released commemorative coins. The coins released were in the denomination of Rupees 100 and Rupee five with Jamsetji Tata's face on it — an honour that no other business man has received to date.

The group operates globally with the purpose **"To improve the quality of life of the communities they serve globally, through long-term stakeholder value creation based on Leadership with Trust"**. The ethos of the group can be found in the words of Chairman Emeritus, Ratan N. Tata, "Business, as I have seen it, places one great demand on you: it needs you to self-impose a framework of ethics, values, fairness and objectivity on yourself at all times". The Tata Group has always been a values-driven organization. These values continue to direct the growth and business of Tata companies. The five core Tata values underpinning the way a Tata entity conducts itself are: (i) Integrity — fair, honest, transparent and ethical in their conduct; everything they do must stand the test of public scrutiny; (ii) Responsibility — integrating the environmental and social principles in their businesses, ensuring that what comes from the people goes back to the people many times over; (iii) Excellence — being passionate about achieving the highest standards of quality, always promoting meritocracy; (iv) Pioneering — being bold and agile, courageously taking on challenges, using deep customer insight to develop innovative solutions and (v) Unity — investing in their people and partners, enabling continuous learning, and building caring and collaborative relationships based on trust and mutual respect.

ARTICULATE

Tata companies have consistently adhered to the values and ideals articulated by the founder for over 150 years. These values and ideals form the foundation on which the Tata Code of Conduct is built. The Tata Code of Conduct is a comprehensive document that serves as the ethical road map for Tata employees and companies. Formalized by Mr. Ratan Tata, the Tata Code of Conduct (TCoC) articulates the group's values and ideals that guide and govern the conduct of their member companies as well as every Tata employee in all matters relating to business. The Code outlines the commitment to each of their stakeholders, including the communities in which they operate, and serves as the guiding light when a Tata leader is faced with business dilemmas and is caught at ethical crossroads. The Code is also reviewed and revised, to maintain its contemporaneity and relevance in geographies. However, it remains unaltered at its core. Not only is a Tata employee expected to follow the code and comply with the laws and regulations around the world, he/she is encouraged to contribute in setting new standards of ethical conduct that will generate deep respect and inspire emulation by others.

The Tatas belong to the small group of companies around the world who think and act first as a corporate citizen of the country they operate in. This citizenship view is a philosophy associated historically with J.N. Tata. In even those early days, his words vocalized the corporate credo of the group: "In a free enterprise, the community is not just another stakeholder in business, but is, in fact, the very purpose of its existence". At a time in the 19th century when aspects like "purpose", "values", "mission", etc. would have been rare to come by, Tata's founder knew exactly what would remain as the core of their businesses and espoused it very clearly.

According to Mr. K.V. Rao, Resident Director for ASEAN for Tata Sons:

"The purpose of Tata is not just a statement that hangs on the wall, but something that is ingrained and is an integral part of the practice culture of all employees. Leadership behaviors are very infectious and when you walk the talk, people believe in what you say. When you start becoming part of that walk, then you start taking personal joy and satisfaction in giving back and that unleashes a virtuous cycle, and this DNA becomes the part of the core. If you have been a TATA employee, you will realize it's just not about the talk from the day that you join our company but a living reality that you experience all the time. Most employees are looking for a larger purpose and understanding better "why they are doing, what they are doing" — it's a delightful journey".

The Tata family has always believed that they must give back to the community and many Tata leaders who were at the helm in the early years put their returns and dividends that came their way into trusts. The Tata Trusts, which own about 2/3 of the Tata group at the holding level, are all public charitable trusts with the objective to serve for the benefit of the community. While a portion of the profit and dividends from a Tata enterprise goes back to public shareholders and institutional investors, a significant portion also goes back to the Trusts and gets invested back into the society. Thus, the Tata group maintains its purpose of giving back to the community, and its unique structure ensures the implementation of its mission of developing the community.

The Tata Group has been a pioneer in Employee Welfare and this is beautifully illustrated in a story of Jamsetji, who visited Manchester, UK, to study the textile mills there in late 1800s. Tata mentioned in his memoirs how he found the mills and working conditions for workers far from satisfactory. He noted how there were no masks for the workers and how women were going to work leaving behind their little children. He also observed how cotton flint would go up the workers' nostrils while they were at work in a stuffy and hot factory, ultimately resulting in poor health for the factory workers in the UK. When Tata opened its first textile mill in Nagpur, India, Jamsetji installed the first humidifiers and fire-sprinklers in India. In 1886, he instituted a Pension Fund, and in 1895 began to pay accident compensation. He was decades ahead of his time and miles ahead of his competitors. This showed that not only profits but people mattered to him.

Even as he battled for the survival of his industry, he was not too busy to think of the health of his workers. As polluted water was a cause of illness, he installed a water filtration plant and arranged for sanitary hutments. A grain depot was opened, followed by a dispensary, provident fund and pension schemes. In those early years, he also introduced a system of apprenticeship. This took place at a time when India was under British rule and no formal labor laws existed and the Factories Act was not even on the radar.

ASSIMILATE

The culture of giving back to the community is central to all Tata companies. Mr. Rao explained:

"Whenever there is a natural disaster, the Tatas rise to the occasion and offer help. This kind of volunteering spirit only comes when it becomes a very active culture, and cultures take time to take root and build. Cultures have a lot to do with chemistry, fluidity, where "good behavior" replicates itself into various things. This is the softer side, why employees want to volunteer and give back. The other side is the structure — when you have a mission, vision, and goals, and you want to make it an organization-wide culture, it is also important to have proper systems and structures. Tatas are unique in the way the ownership structure is made up — perhaps the only one in the world. This unique structure gives us a very strong backing and power to embody our purpose and live it every day. Over the years a system of platforms and programs have been evolved by the Tata companies to ensure proper execution and delivery of the good intents".

The unique Tata structure that Mr. Rao alluded to was the 100+ operating companies, 30+ listed companies and the innumerable corporate entities and subsidiaries under the Tata umbrella. With over 720,000 people in 130 countries and 80–85 nationalities working for the Tata Group, cascading the purpose across different companies and geographies may come across as a tall order. However, it has not been very difficult for the Tatas. What makes Tatas unique is the holding company — Tata Sons. Tata Sons centrally manages the Tata brand and manages some key aspects of the group under federal structure, where the companies are independent and board managed. Tata Sons keeps the herd together, upkeeping the principles of the group and ensuring that every employee is guided to work in line with the Tata Code of Conduct

The governance philosophy adopted by the Tata leadership team is this: "Corporate enterprises must be managed not merely in the interests of their owners, but equally in those of their employees, of the consumers of their products, of the local community and finally of the country as a whole" (JRD Tata, 1973). The Tata philosophy therefore ensures a fair, transparent, accountable and ethical management that protects the interests of all stakeholders, including shareholders, employees, customers, vendors, regulators and society. This is something where Tata Sons follows the laws of the land in letter and spirit and goes beyond mere compliance to highlight desired behaviors and norms of Tata group operating companies.

Elaborating on the role of Tata Sons as a conscience keeper, Mr. Rao explained,

"Conscience keeper role is a very important and a sensitive one — with our multicultural workforces and the countries that we work in, it is important to sensitize, constantly reinforce our core values. In some geographies, some compromises can be termed as "it's a done thing" — and "it goes here". The Tata Sons group offices work with all the Tata Cos subsidiaries and entities all over and promote this culture and encourage local employees to imbibe the same Tata values. This has been our philosophy since the company was established and there will be no deviation from this". Mr. Rao is a firm believer in doing good. He elaborated that, if one undertakes a good deed, it starts multiplying itself multifold.

Resilience has proven to be another governance philosophy at Tata Sons. Business globally has become complex, virtual and interdependent. This is where the building of a sustainable and resilient enterprises is important to Tata Sons. Every company that uses the "Tata" brand is a signatory to the Tata Sons' Brand Equity and Business Promotion (BEBP) agreement. As per this agreement, every Tata company has to adhere to the Tata Code of Conduct (TCoC) and the Tata Business Excellency Model (TBEM).

While the TCoC provides an ethical road map for Tata employees and companies, The TBEM, on the other hand, promotes business excellence in the Tata group companies by bringing in best-in-class processes and facilitating their sharing and adaptation for quicker learning and results. Assessments are conducted by trained and certified assessors in the group companies to assess the process maturity levels of each company and overall performance. The TBEM criteria include the deployment of business practices for excellence in leadership and strategy as well as operational excellence. It reviews the approaches by which the company understands its customers and employees and examines the usage of data systems to measure, analyze and generate reusable knowledge assets. In addition to corroborating the company's strengths and practices, TBEM identifies opportunities for improvement and imperatives to enhance business performance.

ACTIVATE

Community development and support are central to all Tata companies. Each company undertakes long-term projects to help the development and sustainability of the communities around it. These efforts span a wide area including Girl child education, women empowerment, health and sanitation, water conservation, social entrepreneurship, supporting local arts and crafts, environment sustainability and many more. Addressing the needs, issues and problems of the local community drives the companies to carry on these projects and provide long-term sustainable solutions to the community. The Tata Memorial Hospitals, Tata Tata Water Mission, the Okhai brand are just a few examples of the community work done by the Tata companies.

The Tata group has always been quick to support relief efforts during a humanitarian crisis, with a focus on building capacity and resilience in the impacted communities for long-term rehabilitation. They also foster the exchange of ideas that benefit group companies to respond more effectively during disasters. Mr. Rao explained:

"Whenever there is a disaster like cyclone, earthquake, tsunami, etc., we have almost 75000–100000 volunteers, who are trained and ready to come forward. Very often, when disasters happen in Asia, I've been asked if there's any help we can offer and all the Tata companies actually come together to outline our "response strategy". Each of our companies offers specific skills — someone is in IT, and data, someone is in telecommunications, someone is in catering, etc. We combine our resources and the Tata Response Cell under the Tata Sustainability Group leads the efforts to render the necessary services".

Relief, response and rehabilitation efforts have included in-kind donations, support to government relief programs, distribution of relief materials, infrastructure improvements and livelihood promotion and training. In addition, Disaster Response Guidelines have been developed and widely disseminated. The State Disaster Management Teams meet quarterly to exchange information and share good practices.

The current COVID-19 pandemic has piled immense burdens on every nation's healthcare system, leaving millions (including frontline health workers) at risk of exposure. Calling the COVID-19 crisis "one of the toughest challenges that the human race will face", the Tata group has committed a sum of Rs 1,500 crores for the purchase of protective equipment for medical personnel on the frontline, respiratory systems and testing kits to increase per capita testing. The fund was also channeled towards modular treatment facilities for infected patients as well as the training of healthcare workers and the general public. In addition, the group opened the doors of its luxury hotels to doctors and nurses working on the frontlines. The Taj Public Service Welfare Trust also collaborated with renowned Indian celebrity chef Sanjeev Kapoor to provide nutritious meals to doctors and staff at hospitals.

When COVID-19 struck, the first reassurance came from the group Chairman Mr. N Chandrasekharan, that all our employees including contract staff will be taken care of. Similarly when Mr. Rao chaired the meeting with the senior leaders of Tata companies in the ASEAN region when the pandemic started, the 40+ subsidiaries' heads first updated on the health and safety of its employees and families. It is clear from these instances that in the minds of Tata's leaders, employee well-being and safety comes first during a crisis, business follows. This is what is expected of a Tata leader.

In 2008, when the Taj Mahal Palace Hotel in Mumbai was attacked by terrorists, the employees of the Taj Mahal Palace Hotel (which is owned by IHCL, a Tata Group company) put the well-being of their guests above their own safety. Many guests who were at the hotel later remarked how the employees rose to the occasion to protect the guests in the hotel without regard for personal safety. It was the staff's quick thinking that averted many casualties. For example, they rushed hotel guests to safe locations such as kitchens and basements. Telephone operators stayed at their posts, alerting guests to lock doors and not step out of their rooms. Kitchen staff formed human shields to protect guests during evacuation attempts. A few employees lost their lives in helping between 1,200 and 1,500 guests escape. According to a Harvard Business Review article, "The Ordinary Heroes of the Taj" (2011) the Taj employees' actions weren't prescribed in manuals; nor were there any official policies or procedures that existed for such an event.

In another incident in 2004, a tsunami ripped across the Indian Ocean, wreaking havoc on coastal populations from Indonesia to India, killing about 185,000 people. The tidal waves devastated two Taj properties. During the crisis, the Taj staff displayed composure and optimism as they calmed and comforted the panic-stricken guests. With kitchens and store rooms inundated, it was the kitchen staff who salvaged food supplies and carried cooking equipment to higher ground so that they could prepare hot meals for their guest. These two incidents show how Tata employees follow the call of duty and put customers over self.

Even in normal times, the Tata Sustainability Group runs the Tata Engage program, which brings together Tata companies on a common volunteering platform. This umbrella program aims to encourage Tata volunteers around the world to help enrich the community by contributing their time and skills. As of May 2020, the Tata Engage platform had over 75,000 registered volunteers. These volunteers train under the aegis of the Tata Sustainability Group and provide immediate technical assistance in the aftermath of any disaster. Across the Tata offices, employees are also encouraged to volunteer for causes close to their heart. This is not mandated, but highly encouraged. Employees are free to choose what they prefer, be it sports, art, music or social welfare. An employee can raise a formal proposal for a period of full-time volunteering, in an area of their interest. If approved, their salaries are still paid while they are away from the office working on something that is benefitting society. While these opportunities are explicitly for Tata employees, the company does have programs that are targeted at the general public. An example is the TATA marathon that takes place in the US and in India. By providing a platform for so many different people to come together, Tata sends an important message about its inclusiveness and focus on society at large.

CONCLUSION

With each generation, the Tatas have nurtured and improved their capabilities in "stakeholder management": that is, basing their investments and business decisions on the needs and interests of those who are affected in the community they operate in. Since its founding in 1868, Tata has operated on the premise that a company thrives on social capital (i.e. the value created from investing in good community and human relationships) as much as tangible assets for sustainable growth. For the company, this means serving the needs of shareholders, employees, customers and the people of the countries where it operates. In short, Tata's leaders believe the group can survive on the world stage only by being both "too big to beat and too good to fail". In the end, Tata's leaders and executives stick by the familiar argument that doing well by doing good is simply good business. They conduct business the way they do not because they have clear evidence it has a better chance of success, but because they know no other way. The financial sustainability of the group's unique business model could provide a lasting model for other companies that seek to serve new markets and maintain growth, while building a strong reputation as global citizens and fulfilling their own purpose.

Mr. R Gopalakrishnan, a senior Tata leader who served the group as its Executive Director, once said, "We are hard-nosed business guys, who like to earn an extra buck as much as the next guy because we know that extra buck will go back to wipe away a tear somewhere". Tata companies balance their outlook on social benefits and strategies for growth in their businesses without forgetting their philanthropic and fiduciary commitments.

India's post-independence history is intertwined with Tata's support in nation building. The long legacy of the group has led to the establishment of strong connections with governments, public institutions, universities, like-minded corporations and industrial associations. For anyone living in India, it would be unimaginable that he or she would not have been inspired by the Tata brand, which is synonymous with trust. This is the simple reason why the Tata brand has a priceless value attached to it.

13. The Kellogg Co (Kellogg's): *Nourishing Families So They Can Flourish and Thrive*

INTRODUCTION

More than 100 years ago, W.K. Kellogg founded Kellogg Company through his belief in nutrition and dedication to well-being. Motivated by a passion for people, quality and innovation, W.K. created the first-ever breakfast cereal, shaping an entire industry and becoming a household name.

From its earliest days, Kellogg has been a purpose-driven organization. W.K. was an early conservationist, leading philanthropist and a well-being visionary. He instilled in the company the understanding that a critical part of running a good business is also doing good for society. That's why Kellogg has worked hard to make sure that its company and business practices deliver benefits to people, communities and the planet. This is captured in its purpose statement **"nourishing families so they can flourish and thrive"**.

Through its *Kellogg's® Better Days* global purpose the company is committed to driving growth through addressing the interconnected issues of well-being, food security and climate to help end hunger and create better days for three billion people by the end of 2030, by:

- Nourishing People with our Foods
- Feeding People in Need

- Nurturing People and Our Planet
- Living Our Founder's Values

Collectively, these commitments contribute to five of the United Nations Sustainable Development Goals (SDGs).

ARTICULATE

In Asia, Kellogg saw that it could articulate its purpose of "nourishing families so they can flourish and thrive" in the unique role it can play to address hidden hunger in the community. Nutrient deficiency among children is an endemic problem in developing Asian countries such as India. While almost 40% of children in this region are suffering from hidden hunger, Asian mothers don't even see it as a marker of malnutrition. Shekar Khosla, Kellogg's Chief Commercial Officer for Australasia, Middle East and Africa, sees the challenge as a responsibility and an opportunity for the company:

> *Mr.W. K. Kellogg understood that if his mission was to take hold, it must be based on the newly developing science around macro and micronutrients. He therefore employed nutritionists and scientists to not only advise on the composition of the food but also to measure and monitor its impact in the community. This remains central to the way Kellogg develops and improves foods, but now embracing new scientific insights around the importance of eating a diverse plant-based diet and the critical role of fiber in the diet – all while delivering the specific micronutrients which are deficient in particular regions. For Kellogg's impact is not on the food, but the role that food has in helping people fulfill their potential.*

Khosla adds further:

> *I think if we truly want to have a nation achieve its potential, bridging that nutrient gap is extremely important. And that's*

where we feel we have a potentially unique role to play and get that through our foods, our brand purpose coming to life, and in the many ways that we engage with our consumers. We will have a role to play for the next 100 years, if we are able to make a dent on hidden hunger. That's how we will carry forward the legacy of Mr. Kellogg.

Khosla believes that Kellogg's purpose-driven efforts to address hidden hunger (and more specifically micronutrient deficiencies) among children in Asia is good not just for society but also for the business. He believes that when people start having a particular food at a young age, they become familiar with the food as they grow up and develop a strong affinity for the brand. As he puts it, *"Children are a platform for access into the house from a brand point of view, but the consumption flows to all members of the family and is key to solving the micronutrient deficiencies for all".*

As far as the consumer is concerned, the "face" of Kellogg is its brand and its people. Thus, the company has focused its efforts on expressing purpose through its brand promise ("Helping you be your best. Now, for over 100 years"), its brand content (Kellogg was one of the first companies to print nutrition labeling on its packaging) and its people who are working at the frontline in sales.

Kellogg's purpose has propelled it to the "top 20 brands" on the Purpose Power Index — the largest study ever measuring perceptions of brand purpose, based on more than 17,500 individual ratings among over 7,500 US consumers, and encompassing more than 200 different brands (https://www.purposepowerindex.com).

ASSIMILATE

Although Kellogg stands for many things in the US and its other core markets, it is a relatively young brand in Asia. This presents the company with the opportunity to internally embed the company's purpose in a way that resonates culturally. As Khosla recounted when he joined the company in 2015:

> *One of the first questions we asked was what do we want the brand to stand for? After some work, we came to this brand purpose about nourishing human potential. We felt inspired by that idea and purpose, but as we took that idea for a walk with our finance colleagues, supply chains, HR, R&D, etc., they found an expression of that idea within their own functions. It is ultimately about human potential, and human potential is not defined by functions or hierarchies or territories. Because it is based on human truth, it's embraced by other functions. What this allows us to do is build a campus recruitment program, with a proposition that we have the soul of a start-up. So, if you want to join the mentality of a start-up, but within the security of a large MNC, and want to explore your potential, then Kellogg's is a great place to be.*

Recruitment

The ethos of "nourishing human potential" starts with recruitment — that is, looking for the 'right' values in the people the company hires and doing what it takes to keep those values alive after that person joins. Kellogg values integrity, accountability, passion, humility, simplicity and a focus on success. But it is humility that Khosla highlights. He believes that it is an imperative to have team members who either live (or have lived) the same circumstances as their consumers — this shared background and experience will make it intuitive for them to understand the customer's issues and find solutions for those issues. He explains further:

> *For example, if you're serving base-of-the-pyramid consumers and you have people who have only been brought up in super luxury penthouses and never stepped outside to see what the*

common people do, it'll be hard for them to appreciate. Therefore, that's what I try and do – I try and get people who are hungry and aspirational but have had roots in the dominant cohort of our consumer base, so they can intuitively understand what the needs of our consumers are. It really begins from there, then how you nurture that spirit turns back to humility in many ways.

In addition to ensuring that new hires have values that are aligned with the company's, Kellogg also looks for the requisite leadership, functional and skill-based competencies to make an impact on the issue of "nourishing human potential". Khosla adds from his own experience:

People join Kellogg's for all the things they can do. However, they stay because of all the things they can be. And that is an example of journeying to realize your potential.

Leadership

Purpose is assimilated at Kellogg through leadership by example. Within the company, leadership does not necessarily equate with the C-suite or with seniority. Instead, it is thought leadership that really matters. For example, a leader could be a millennial working in the Pringles business. By giving them opportunities to speak and by providing case studies of what they have accomplished, the company endeavors to give such people more visibility in the organization so they can inspire and influence others. According to Khosla, there is a lot of responsibility on leaders to embody and live the company's purpose through everything they do. This involves a lot of self-check as well as providing coaching and mentoring for the company's young talent.

Work Process

One simple but impactful behavior that Kellogg cultivates has to do with how everyone spends their first 15 minutes at work. For most people, their morning office routine starts with a perusal of their emails. This routine has a tendency to over-focus on urgent rather than on important issues. To address this shortcoming, Kellogg is encouraging its people to make opening their consumer pulse dash boards the first thing they do when they arrive at their office. The impact of this simple action on embedding Kellogg's purpose is elaborated by Khosla:

> *Immediately, in your first 15 minutes of your work day, you're immersing yourself in the world of your consumer, rather than the world of Outlook, which is 99% internal. I think if people start opening the consumer and culture dashboard, it forces you and inspires you to make your day more fulfilling. This is the guiding energy and oxygen for the rest of the day. We're doing a fundamental shift on how people start their day.*

Unlike many global companies, the process of purpose assimilation at Kellogg is less formal and structured and much more "organic". Khosla attributes this to the company's roots in a small town (Battle Creek) in the US Midwest. While appreciating that the "nice", "soft" and "humble" aspects of Kellogg's culture bring many benefits, Khosla believes the company has much to accomplish in the marketplaces, as doing so would translate into better company performance and purpose fulfillment:

> *We have so much to accomplish from a business point of view and to make a real dent on hidden hunger and we have to do it in a way that is uniquely Kellogg's — retaining our belief in doing well by doing good. We cannot accept a win less than 100% as a definition of success. 99% is not a success. How can we keep raising our standards externally and internally in the organization? Whether it's designing better food, better brand experiences, being more demanding of oneself and our partner ecosystem, of the quality and standard of the work we put out there in the market, I think it's getting people to realize we can retain our*

softer inner soul, while making a visible impact in the market, for our customers and in our consumers lives.

ACTIVATE

Kellogg is unique in having a global platform that is dedicated to delivering critical nourishment to three billion people by the end of 2030. Called *Better Days*, the platform is an expression of the company's "four pillars" of feeding people in hunger and need, providing safe and trusted food, doing good for the planet through sustainable initiatives, and living the founder's values. The following section describes how the company is activating its purpose in Asia through each of the "four pillars":

1. Nourish with Our Foods
   - Kellogg Korea launched its #Nutritiongram on Instagram (kelloggsnutrition_kr) to share nutrition information with healthcare professionals in Korea who are interested in health and food. Already, the account has nearly 1,200 followers.
2. Feeding People in Need
   - In Korea, the Good Morning Kellogg program is providing healthy and balanced meals to help fight hunger and nurture the development of youngsters in a childcare facility who have either no families or families with little means.
   - The Healthy Food, Healthy Mind program in Malaysia was a Kellogg pilot program supported by the Food Aid Foundation

and the W.K. Kellogg Institute for Food Nutrition and Research. Twice a week, 100 kindergarten-age children from low- to middle-income families in the outskirts of Nilai, Negeri Sembilan, received information on healthy eating habits. Kellogg also provided milk and fruit to accompany the children's breakfast cereal. Starting in 2019, the program was expanded to reach 326 students, five days a week.

- Working with the Singapore-based ecosystem builder AVPN, Kellogg has built deeper public–private partnerships with organizations to address morning hunger in India, where 70% of children are undernourished.

3. Nurturing Our Planet
   - *Improving livelihoods while reducing environmental impact in India*
     In the central India state of Madhya Pradesh, Kellogg and TechnoServe partnered on a two-and-a-half year, three-phase program to help smallholder farmers improve their livelihoods and resilience to climate change. More than 12,000 farmers received training on three key aspects of climate-smart agriculture: farm productivity, farm resilience and impact of the farm on the environment. 64% of the participants were men who received agronomy training and 36% were women who received training in organic kitchen gardening.

     Over the course of the project, farmers adopted best practices including soil testing, seed germination and use of organic fertilizers that reduced their cost of operations and increased productivity. Sustainable farm revenue increased by more than 20% in the first two phases and by more than 40% in the third phase of the project.

     The organic kitchen gardens continue to improve the overall nutrition of Madhya Pradesh, with 97% of families now consuming vegetables at least twice a day. One-third of the female farmers also started earning extra income by selling their surplus organic vegetables.

The project also promoted collective marketing through Farmer Producer Companies (FPC) formed by farmers that share profits and benefits among the membership. By building the capacity of local farmers, the FPCs are now well-run, sustainable operations with established, value-added supply chains for their wheat, maize, chickpea, soybean and jaggery crops. In less than three years, the program created more than US$4.7 million in incremental, replicable financial benefits to the more than 12,000 participating farmers.

- *Advancing sustainable agriculture: Sourcing potato flakes in Bangladesh*
  As one of the poorest countries in the world, Bangladesh has numerous political, economic, social and environmental challenges. However, Bangladesh is the third largest producer of potatoes in Asia, and potatoes are the second largest agricultural crop in Bangladesh. Since 2014, Kellogg has been working with SEBA Limited to help smallholders improve potato farming methods that increase yields and boost incomes. Today, these farmers' crop yields are 25–100% higher, and they have a steady source of income since Kellogg began purchasing its potatoes for its *Pringles®* plant in Asia.

- *Responsible sourcing of palm oil*
  Although Kellogg uses a very small amount of palm oil globally, it has been working since 2009 to improve the sustainability of its palm oil supply chain. The World Wildlife Fund gave Kellogg a 9 out of 9 for sustainable palm oil production, identifying it as an industry leader in this effort.

All of the palm oil Kellogg uses globally is sourced through a combination of the Roundtable on Sustainable Palm Oil (RSPO) Certified Segregated supply chain, RSPO Mass Balance mixed-source supply chain and the purchase of RSPO Credits. In 2018, CDP gave Kellogg an A- for the last three years for its work ensuring and sourcing sustainable palm oil.

Since 2015, Kellogg has partnered with Proforest to engage its Tier One global palm suppliers in a bi-annual survey to measure traceability, transparency and policy adherence. Currently, 97% of the palm oil it uses globally is traceable to the mill, and 39% is traceable to a specific plantation.

4. Living our Founder's Values
   Some of the values that make up this pillar — especially acting with integrity and accountability — were evident in Kellogg's COVID-19 response. When the pandemic hit Asia, Kellogg took the position that its biggest responsibility was to ensure the availability of its food products to its millions of consumers. According to Khosla, people in Asia already had so much to worry about — being able to find quality food on store shelves should be the last of their concerns. Hence, the company took its responsibility of ensuring adequate food supply to stores across the region very seriously. Moreover, it stuck to its principles and refrained from profiteering, despite the panic buying and the increased purchase of trusted food brands in various Asian markets during the crisis.

To date, Kellogg and its charitable funds have donated more than US$10 million to global COVID-19 hunger relief efforts.

CONCLUSION

The sheer diversity in the cultures and economic conditions of the markets in Asia presents businesses with significant challenges. It is a region that comprises countries with the features of a developed market (e.g. Singapore) as well as countries with the profile of an emerging economy (e.g. Vietnam). Amidst this diversity, it is the corporate purpose that keeps Kellogg's people and brands across the countries oriented towards a common "true north".

What stands out about Kellogg's purpose journey is how it has managed to stay true to its founder's core purpose and values, which date back to more than 100 years. At the same time, it has been able to articulate the purpose with nuances that make it highly relevant to the Asian context (i.e. addressing hidden hunger) and to its own people ("nourishing human potential"), thus fostering its assimilation into the company's culture. Furthermore, its *Better Days* framework ensures that its purpose activation is directed towards achieving big, strategic goals.

Purpose has helped Kellogg to be a successful and sustainable enterprise for more than 100 years. According to Khosla, the company aims to be around for another 100 years, and purpose will continue to be the guide for that unfolding journey.

14. UPS: *Connecting a Global Community Through Intelligent Logistic Networks*

INTRODUCTION

United Parcel Service (UPS) was founded in Seattle, Washington, in 1907 by James E. Casey and was originally named "American Messenger Company". In 1919, American Messenger Company became "United Parcel Service". Within a decade, UPS became the first package delivery company to provide air service via private airlines. UPS also holds the first as a package delivery company to serve every address in the United States by 1975. By 1985, UPS had commenced international air service. It was in 1998 that UPS established its operations in Asia with Singapore as its Asia Pacific headquarters. Today, UPS has close to 13,000 employees in Asia Pacific serving 41 countries and territories in this region. Currently, UPS is the world's largest parcel carrier, and is the largest company in its industry in terms of revenue and profits. UPS believes it is its competitive strategy that has helped it to separate itself from its competitors leading to a competitive advantage in its business model adopted by the company regarding its operations.

With the advance in technology, shrinking of supply chain, global warming, etc., UPS has constantly refocused its way to run its operations to be cost-efficient and contribute to the company's coffers. UPS prides itself on having leveraged on digital technologies like the Delivery Information Acquisition Device (DIAD), which virtually eliminates the use of paper between UPS and the customer and On-Road Integrated Optimization and Navigation (ORION) to help improve the routes drivers use to deliver packages and reduce fuel costs. With a high focus on technology, accessibility and a global footprint, UPS has been able to grow by anchoring its activities on the purpose statement, **"Connect a global community through intelligent logistic networks"**.

ARTICULATE

The values of a UPS employee articulated by its founder, Jim Casey, 113 years ago still remains valid and relevant over a century later. The seven values laid by the founder were (i) Integrity as the core of UPS and in all that it does, (ii) Team work — Determined people working together can accomplish anything, (iii) Service — Serving the needs of its customers and communities as central to its success, (iv) Quality and Efficiency — To remain constructively dissatisfied in its pursuit of excellence, (v) Safety — where the well-being of the UPS employees and business partners and the public is given the utmost importance, (vi) Sustainability — where there is a commitment to contribute to social responsibility and (vii) Innovation — where creativity and change are essential to growth.

UPS holds a reputation for grooming its leaders up the corporate ladder. Many senior level executives from the US hold the privilege of having started on the job as UPS truck drivers' decades ago and now hold leadership positions. Mr. Ross McCullough, President, UPS Asia Region, is someone who began his career with UPS in

1984 while completing his undergraduate studies as a part-time employee.

McCullough shared, "The policies and expected conduct as a UPS employee is something all of us get on the day we become a management person and that is our policy book. Within that is contained a very rich set of descriptions explaining how we deal with our people, the company and the community. It is a very detailed set of policies that have evolved since the founding of the company (first published in 1929). Very often, we start meetings with discussions about policies and interpret the meaning of them, how we're using them today within our company. There are three elements captured within the policy book that contain the essence of our purpose, which is a combination of our mission, our core values and the strategy. This helps us at the leadership level and every employee at UPS to focus our activities on the communities we serve particularly in the midst of this COVID-19 situation. Our strong policies guide us to live our purpose during these difficult times of COVID when we introduced our Business Continuity Plans and the awareness of the role we play as a global logistics company".

Ms. Tanie Eio, Chief Human Resource Officer at UPS for the region, is someone who has been with UPS for the last 19 years. She reaffirmed how the UPS policy book plays a key role in educating every employee on the mission of the company, the values, strategy and purpose. She articulated how one statement from the policy book has had a profound impact on her and still lingers in her mind. The UPS policy book lists out "We Enable Global Commerce". This statement according to Ms Eio contributes to the purpose of why UPS exists as a company since UPS is responsible for the movement of

6–10% of the world's GDP through their network. Within Asia Pacific, Ms Eio was instrumental in drawing up the APAC vision map, which is used in UPS meetings that are aligned with the company's purpose.

McCullough recalled a Corporate document from 2015, which was a launch document that literally detailed using gamification among other engagement techniques to communicate Enterprise Strategy. While this emerged from headquarters, the APAC office of UPS adapted it to Asia. Ms. Eio and her team listed out specific vignettes which were critical to the cultural fabric of UPS based on the overarching values and purpose of UPS. This was followed by highly engaged conversations among the employees to really understand each vignette and what it meant for a UPS employee and how they interpreted it. They discussed at length as to what each vignette meant in the relationship between a UPS employee and its stakeholders. Clear identification of processes and responsibility emerged from these conversations aiding UPS with a clear "Live It Framework" for future actions. These discussions and vignettes have been depicted in what is called the Vision Map for UPS APAC. Such conversations and activities were cascaded across the various offices in the region with formal launch ceremonies helping UPS to be agile and adaptable to embed their purpose into the minds and hearts of each UPS hero whereever they may be. The Vision Map has four parts to it. (i) Communications — Telling the story using the Vision Map Discussion Guide, use of interactive vision map, videos, shout outs and town hall meetings. (ii) Hype — Generating Interest through Apps, Board Games, Viral Campaign, Contests, Prizes and Swag creation. (iii) Training — Equipping and empowering the employees with Deep Dive Training, Ambassador Tool Kit, Instructor Led Learning, Tools for Daily Work and hands on workshops. (iv) Infrastructure — Walking the Talk through Idea collection platform, Accelerated Approvals, Listening Tours and Sharing of Success Stories.

APAC Vision Map

We are UPS Asia Pacific

UPS APAC is committed to being the region's leading logistics service provider, connecting global communities through intelligent and sustainable logistics networks. We are United Problem Solvers, helping our customers discover new opportunities for growth. We take ownership of our strategy and continuously develop ourselves to achieve our objectives.

Connect. Create. Change.

SAFETY INTEGRITY WELLNESS INNOVATION DIVERSITY & INCLUSION SERVICE RESPECT QUALITY TEAMWORK EFFICIENCY SUSTAINABILITY

EMPOWERED
We take personal responsibility for our work, making informed decisions to deliver an excellent customer experience and grow our business.

AGILE
We maintain a sense of urgency in serving our customers. We solve problems quickly and effectively, driving customer satisfaction and brand loyalty.

INNOVATIVE
We create opportunities for the future by questioning the status quo. We recognize and embrace the pace of change as a way to go further for our customers and our company.

We are UPS Heroes

OUR PATH FORWARD

Develop Our People

Achieve Balanced Growth

Excel Service

Deliver Exceptional Customer Experience

Leverage Our Network for Future Growth

This meticulously created vision map which is depicted above has helped UPS APAC to empower its employees and come up with innovative ideas to guide their actions thereby assimilating the sense of purpose in their actions. China was first of the countries to experience COVID. In January 2020, UPS airlifted for free more than 2 million respirator masks, 280,000 pairs of nitrile gloves and 11,000 protective gears to China to combat the spread of corona virus in Wuhan, China, in coordination with the Red Cross Society in China. During these challenging times, UPS lived and showed the rest of the world their commitment to their purpose — connecting a global community through intelligent logistics networks.

ASSIMILATE

Ross McCullough took over as APAC President in 2016. In the last four years at the helm of Asia-Pacific, McCullough observed, "Our people have stepped up remarkably to all the challenges by living and exemplifying our values of protecting our people and defending the reputation of our company. Our purpose to serve the global community is so strong and embedded within our culture. Every UPS employee knows this. Indeed, it is a complicated formula internally but during periods like the current times (COVID-19), due to the way we have ingrained this across our various offices, it stands brightly. My colleagues in Asia stepped up to this remarkable challenge of COVID, protecting our people and our company. In the initial weeks we focused on China and then spread out to serve the PPE needs around the world. You can't train these things; they are embedded within the culture. We live the things that are laid out in the policy, the mission, the vision for the company, the core values and the strategy. All this leads to UPS living up to the purpose of 'connecting a global community through intelligent logistics'".

Referring to the Vision Map of UPS that has helped UPS live up to its Purpose statement, Ms. Eio shared, "The top left in our vision map explains where we want to be as the leading logistics provider within the region. The way the map is created is such that we anticipate the world is changing, and if we don't adapt or disrupt ourselves, the outside world will disrupt us. With that in mind we asked ourselves what we could do differently in the way we run our business, in the way we look at our processes and the way we conduct ourselves. This map is not the result of detailed research done externally and internally, but it's vision set by APAC UPSers for APAC UPSers. We involved our millennial employees in the creation of the map and they contributed to the "connect, create, change" slogan. We also had various departments share their impression of future UPS. While we can set the best vision for any company, without the right people we can't get there. We expect our leaders to create an environment for people to thrive and be successful, at the same time, our rank and file employees are given the opportunity to demonstrate their capabilities and explore the new culture we are setting for the company. Everyone's voice is important".

As further explanation as to how UPS has assimilated its purpose into its activities, McCullough shared a recent incident from China. A UPS driver from the China office was one of the first employees to have caught the corona virus. Once the employee had gotten better and was still serving his quarantine period in the hospital, he delivered food and mail to patients within the facility. The office stayed connected with him capturing the stories of how he used to spend his day and the support he was extending to his fellow patients. When the office in Wuhan opened after close to two months of being shut down, they had more packages in one day than they had in the month before. UPS was unable to find a company to disinfect the facility before opening it. This is where the employees from the centre management team volunteered their own time to go in and disinfect the operation to make sure every employee getting back to the office felt safe and secure. McCullough also recalled how his colleagues from the Shenzhen Hub went out of the way to retrieve 400 packages of critical healthcare equipment among hundreds and thousands of packages that needed to be delivered to hospitals during the lockdown period. Since the regular supply chain operations were impacted, the Shenzhen team collaborated with a local partner in China to get those packages delivered to the hospital. UPS pilots and crew volunteered to fly into China with Personal Protective Equipment (PPE) at a time when people were wary and cautious of flying into China. These acts from the UPS heroes exemplify their behavior, which McCullough believes has been embedded in their DNA. With the focus on empowerment that Ms. Eio highlighted, there is enough evidence that UPS heroes are empowered to do the right things without somebody telling them what to do.

To this end, UPS APAC offices take great pains to record every single event, life story, achievements, and success stories of any accomplishments that will showcase the components of this map. The UPS brand name in the US and even Europe are traditionally associated with the children getting their Christmas gifts and a fond association with the brand. Asia does not enjoy the same level of parity with the US in terms of brand name and McCullough and Eio are working towards changing this mindset. Ms Eio remarked, "Our efforts for activating the UPS purpose are evident from the term 'UPS Heroes' so as to instill the importance and significance of each employee feeling proud about the work they do and to be at an equal footing with a UPS driver in the US and Europe. In general, Asians are more reserved, don't speak up as much, and we tend to undermine our own abilities. To make it worse, our leaders are not very pro-active when it comes to recognizing our people. We are making conscious efforts to get away from this mindset because we believe that every one of our employees here in Asia are good contributors. In fact, some are even better than world talents that we have seen. The fact remains that somehow they are not given the platform to flourish. By coining the term, 'UPS Heroes', we want to showcase them and make them visible — not just within the Asia-Pac, but to the world. We are not there yet, but at least that is the vision we want to head towards — and we need our leaders, especially Asian leaders and global UPS leaders, to recognize that and to enable our people to shine. The more efforts we put into this, the more heroes we create from Asia to propel our purpose of connecting a global community through intelligent logistic networks".

ACTIVATE

As UPS connects a global community through its intelligent logistics networks, it continues to invest in technology, be it physical assets like its airplanes, and it looks into the automation in its hubs, to link the entire supplier chain across the world. To assimilate the core of its purpose into its actions, UPS understands the significance of collaboration as a critical aspect that can let it achieve its purpose and link employees with the various stakeholders in its ecosystem.

UPS capitalizes on technology to help its employees collaborate. Telephone calls, spreadsheets, documents and e-mails are exchanged daily to help not only the employees within one location, but worldwide with closed-loop feedback to be shared with the sender as to whether or not the message was received. While this may sound rudimentary for most business operations, in the case of the UPS business, delivery changes can be impacted dramatically if all parties do not collaborate leading to UPS losing its stronghold in the business. Drivers on the road use the DIAD to collaborate with dispatchers who receive the delivery information. The dispatchers can also alert the drivers where to deliver by using the DIAD and if the message is not received or is given incorrectly,

UPS could once again lose business. Not only do these processes require feedback, but the use of the technology requires feedback as well. UPS therefore invites constant feedback from those parties using the technology to point out any deficiencies or improvizations that can be made to optimize technology. Iteration of the processes and the constant repetition helps a UPS employee to not only understand the outcomes but also the consequences of how it works and the basic expectations from each employee.

UPS from an external perspective runs like a well-oiled machine. It has been in APAC for more than three decades. Hence a lot of models, frameworks, processes are from the US but adapted to the unique APAC environment. The APAC team felt the need to curate a distinct identity for themselves in their operations, in their processes and lending their own voice to create a culture without compromising on the values, strategies and mission espoused by the founder.

McCullough added how UPS emphasizes on actions and outcomes, not words. While words are certainly important, McCullough believes that it is the actions that carry weight. To that end, McCullough was instrumental in promoting a number of APAC talent to the highest-level jobs in the 32 year history of UPS in Asia. A quick scan on the APAC leadership team at UPS is a testimony of this initiative.

The vision map of UPS also highlights sustainability as one of the visions to achieve its purpose. As the largest package delivery company in the world, it is constantly asking itself how to be a more sustainable company. It has a huge fleet of aircraft and flying these aircraft adds to the carbon footprint. It has committed to bringing down the impact of its carbon output. UPS is proud of its Boeing B747-8F fleet, considered to be the most fuel-efficient four-engine aircraft in the world, 15 of which were deployed in Asia in 2019. UPS has also consciously planted trees in the communities it operates in towards greening the environment. Since 2012, UPS employees have planted 15.4 million trees surpassing their goal of planting 15 million trees by 2020. The company also prepares a robust global sustainability report on the impact of its business reviewing its commitments to the environment and the communities it serves.

As an enabler of the global supply chain, UPS recognizes that what it does also impacts the carbon footprint of its customers. It is only natural therefore that its customers expect it to bring solutions that help reduce their emissions. The UPS portfolio of sustainability solutions are aimed at helping UPS's customers — big or small — to measure, manage and mitigate the transportation impact of its supply chain, whether it's around the world or around the corner. UPS has also been relentless in its pursuit of efficiency and innovation, where it is building the smart logistics network of the future. By investing in alternative fuel and advanced technology vehicles, and expanding the use of renewable energy to reduce the environmental impact of its operations, UPS has contributed to reducing its emissions across its operations, while staying true to its purpose of "connecting a global community through intelligent logistics networks".

Having experienced SARS, the UPS team has been able to react proactively to COVID. UPS took a call that no matter how much the PPEs were going to cost it, it would procure them and deliver them to all its employees so that they can be protected. UPS demonstrated upholding its values of team work, safety, quality and efficiency. It also upheld its mission of growing its global business by serving the logistics needs of customers, offering excellence and value in all that it does, keeping in mind the broad ownership by the employees and leading by example as a responsible, caring and a sustainable company. These actions of UPS has made it anchor its business on the purpose of connecting a global community through intelligent logistics networks.

CONCLUSION

The UPS APAC team is sitting on the shoulder of giants — US and Europe — where there is a larger legacy in the number of years it has been in business. The leadership in APAC has managed to stay rooted in the values set by their founder and crafted a purpose for Asia aligned with the mission and vision of UPS. Aligned with their purpose, Ross McCullough took on the most important decision during these challenging times. Despite the economic downturn due to COVID, the Asia office decided to go ahead with the annual increments to their people who had tirelessly worked so hard in the past months. Literally everyone in the company had done something extra. Having been classified as providing essential services, every UPS Hero had gone beyond their call of duty to live up to their purpose of connecting the community through intelligent logistics. This action from the leadership is a way to demonstrate to the larger team that the UPS Heroes are an integral part of the team and the organization will take care of them despite the circumstances. From this chapter on UPS, the reader can deduce how the long history of a company with its values, missions and strategies has enabled the current leaders to weave a purpose embedding these foundational values to power on.

Conclusion

The 13 companies featured in this book represent different developmental stages in a company's purpose-led journey. We have classified the three stages as *emerging, evolutionary* and *established*. Companies in the emerging stage are those that have had to develop their purpose *from scratch* in the past few years. *Evolutionary*-stage companies have had to redefine their original purpose in response to external or internal catalysts, such as a change in strategy (DSM), the competitive landscape (DBS) or internationalization (Mahindra). Last but not least, companies in the *established* stage mostly comprise legacy companies that have stayed faithful to the purpose of their legendary founders (e.g. BD, Kellogg, Kova and Tata).

Our case analysis of the 13 companies also reveals three broad categories of approaches in developing purpose, which we have classified as *bottom-up, top-down* and *hybrid* (i.e. combining both top-down and bottom-up approaches).

In addition, we have classified each company according to whether they used a retrospective or prospective approach (Malnight *et al.*, 2019) in developing their purpose. The retrospective approach is internally focused on making sense of the company's history and codifying its cultural DNA to (re)discover its reason for being. On the other hand, the prospective approach is externally focused on changes in the broader ecosystem and assessing the company's potential impact on it, so as to redefine its reason for being (Malnight *et al.*, 2019).

	Emerging	Evolutionary	Established	Bottom-up	Hybrid	Top-down	R/P
BD			X			X	R
DBS		X				X	P
DSM		X				X	P
Kellogg			X			X	R
Kova			X			X	R
LIXIL	X				X		P
Mahindra		X				X	P
Olam		X			X		P
Prudential	X				X		P
Red Hat			X	X			P
Siemens	X				X		P
Tata			X			X	R
UPS			X		X		R

Notes: Key: R = Retrospective approach; P = Prospective approach.

The companies that belong to the *emerging* stage — i.e. LIXIL, Prudential and Siemens Smart Infrastructure — used a *hybrid, prospective* approach. In each case, the company was formulating its purpose for the very first time, as it was either a brand new organization (Siemens Smart Infrastructure) or one that sought to create a new or separate organizational identity (LIXIL and Prudential). In all three cases, there was little or no legacy purpose to constrain them.

The four companies that belong to the *evolutionary* stage — DBS, DSM, Mahindra and Olam — unanimously adopted a prospective approach, as they were redefining their purpose in response to unfolding opportunities or challenges in their operating environment, such as changes in societal needs and expectations and technological developments.

It is perhaps no coincidence that companies with a long-*established* purpose are associated with legendary founders — most notably

Jamsetji Tata (Tata), Maxwell Becton and Fairleigh Dickinson (BD), Dr. W.K. Kellogg (Kellogg) and Dr. Nguyen Thi Hoe (Kova) — whose individual visions drove the definition of the company's purpose. Among our 13 cases, an *established* purpose is typically developed using *top-down* and *retrospective* approaches. Red Hat is an anomaly, as it has a core value proposition (i.e. open-source technology) that almost *demands* that its purpose be developed using a bottom-up, prospective approach. Such companies are rare.

If you have made it this far in the book, we hope you are already convinced that a well-defined purpose can help people in your company understand the "why", the "what" and the "how" of your business (Malnight *et al.*, 2019). However, a word of caution is in order: the same skepticism that has surrounded some companies and their corporate social responsibility (CSR) is starting to emerge for corporate purpose. Stakeholders feel that some companies are jumping on the purpose bandwagon for PR and marketing purposes or to divert public attention away from controversial practices. The Pepsi debacle provides a cautionary tale: In 2017, a Pepsi ad featuring US celebrity Kendall Jenner joining a peace march and handing a police officer a can of Pepsi provoked a fierce backlash. So, instead of burnishing a company's reputation, corporate purpose can backfire in a big way.

Articulating a company's purpose is just the first step towards actualizing it — the purpose still needs to be assimilated into the company's culture and translated into tangible actions and commitments that must satisfy stakeholders' scrutiny. The purpose-driven journeys of the 13 companies featured in this book offer leaders four key lessons:

1. **Your purpose must be unique:** Red Hat "exists to promote openness — to be a champion for collaboration, sharing and transparency in the world". It has the distinction of being the

first software company in the world to own the "open" philosophy. Kova was founded to "provide Vietnamese people with sustainable and affordable living environments through science-based products". The uniqueness of its purpose stems from the specificity of its consumer benefit and its geographical focus. UPS' purpose "to connect a global network through intelligent logistic networks" leverages its unique strengths.

2. **Your purpose must address real issues that your key stakeholders are facing:** Kellogg's purpose of "nourishing families so they can flourish and thrive" is aimed at solving hidden hunger in the communities in which it operates. DBS' purpose of "making banking joyful" captures its endeavor of making banking less of a chore for consumers in the digital economy. And Prudential's purpose of "innovating to help everyone live well" revolves around the need to address the challenges and opportunities experienced by people living longer lives.

3. **Your purpose must inspire and be believed by the people in your company:** BD's purpose of "advancing the world of health" is embodied in the employees who went beyond the call of duty to help their community and stakeholders combat COVID-19. Through its "Re-imagine" workshops and 500 "re-imagineers", Olam created a sense of openness and belonging among its people and generated innovative ideas. The personal sacrifices made by staff of the Taj Mahal Palace Hotel in Mumbai in the 2008 terrorist attack are powerful testimonies to Tata's purpose of "improving the life of the communities they serve globally".

4. **Your purpose must achieve demonstrable impact through its activation:** LIXIL activated its purpose of "making better homes a reality for everyone, everywhere" by developing its SATO range of toilets for people belonging to the base of the pyramid. Mahindra extended loans to the "unbankable" and gave them the ability to earn an income and use that income to repay the loan. Siemens' tripartite partnership in rural India will ultimately create carbon-free, reliable and sustainable power supply for thousands of villages. DSM's Smart Farm initiative

has shown early success in producing optimized yields and reduced emissions in value chains through precision nutrition.

A CALL TO ACTION

All the companies featured in this book have remained remarkably stable during the COVID-19 crisis, as their purpose has helped them to navigate the unprecedented challenges by serving as a guiding light. We would like to conclude our book by issuing you a call to action, which we have translated into prompts in the following worksheet. The answers you provide to these questions can help to ensure that you articulate, assimilate and activate a powerful purpose for your company. May your purpose-driven journey be an exciting and rewarding one!

ARTICULATE

1. Are you convinced that having a well-articulated purpose is critical to the future of your company?
2. Do you have an existing purpose?
3. Is it clearly, succinctly and memorably articulated?
4. Does it hit the 'sweet spot' between your company's heritage, core competencies and values, and stakeholder needs and expectations?
5. Is your purpose still relevant in today's times?
6. Have you identified the mega trends that will have an impact on your business?[1]
7. What role can you play in the ecosystem that will offer new opportunities for your company in the future?[2]
8. What new needs, opportunities and challenges lie ahead for your company and your stakeholders?[3]

---

[1] Malnight *et al.* (2019).
[2] *Ibid.*
[3] *Ibid.*

ASSIMILATE

1. Is your purpose formally aligned with your strategy? If not, what actions can you take to start a conversation about it?
2. Is a person's alignment with purpose used as a criterion for hiring and promotion? If not, how can your company incorporate purpose into your hiring and promotion processes?
3. What reward or incentives are already in place (or need to be in place) to foster the assimilation of purpose?
4. What training or forums are already in place (or need to be in place) to foster the assimilation of purpose?
5. To what extent does your company's leadership team "talk the talk" and "walk the walk"? That is, to what degree do they demonstrate through their words and actions the primacy and meaning of the purpose? What can the company do to further encourage this?
6. What communication channels or platforms do you already have in place (or need to be in place) to facilitate formal and informal discussions between leaders and employees (and among employees) on purpose-related matters?
7. What tangible examples are there on how the purpose has been assimilated within the cultural fabric of the company?
8. What business impacts has your company seen in response to its decision to embrace a purpose-led culture?

ACTIVATE

1. Has your company already identified the focal areas in which your purpose can be activated? Are these focal areas aligned with the company's core competencies and key stakeholder/community/societal needs?
2. Does your company have a sound set of criteria for selecting external partners who can help to activate your purpose and achieve the desired impact?

3. Does your company have the talent and the resources to ensure that activation initiatives are competently managed and followed through?
4. Do you have KPIs to assess the effectiveness of your activation?
5. Do your external stakeholders recognize you as a purpose-led company?
6. Has leading by purpose given you an edge in your industry when compared to your competitors?

REFERENCE

Malnight, T.W., Buche, I., and Dhanaraj, C. (2019). Put purpose at the core of your strategy. *Harvard Business Review*. Available at: https://hbr.org/2019/09/put-purpose-at-the-core-of-your-strategy.

Printed in the United States
by Baker & Taylor Publisher Services